Making Economic Policy

CARL LIEBERMAN

The University of Akron

PRENTICE HALL, INC., *Englewood Cliffs, New Jersey 07632*

Library of Congress Cataloging-in-Publication Data

Lieberman, Carl (date)
Making economic policy / by Carl Lieberman.
p. cm.

Includes bibliographical references and index.
ISBN 0-13-543349-5 (paper)
1. Fiscal policy--United States. 2. Government spending policy--United States. 3. United States--Economic policy. 4. Policy sciences. I. Title.
HJ141.L47 1991
338.973--dc20 90-42464
CIP

Editorial/production supervision and
interior design: ELIZABETH BEST
Cover design: PATRICIA KELLY
Prepress buyer: DEBRA KESAR
Manufacturing buyer: MARY ANN GLORIANDE
Page makeup: JOH LISA

In memory of my brother,
Allan Lieberman

Printed in the United States of America

10 9 8 7 6 5 4 3 2 1

ISBN 0-13-543349-5

Prentice-Hall International (UK) Limited, *London*
Prentice-Hall of Australia Pty. Limited, *Sydney*
Prentice-Hall Canada, Inc., *Toronto*
Prentice-Hall Hispanoamericana, S.A., *Mexico*
Prentice-Hall of India Private Limited, *New Delhi*
Prentice-Hall of Japan, Inc., *Tokyo*
Simon & Schuster Asia Pte. Ltd., *Singapore*
Editora Prentice-Hall do Brasil, Ltda., *Rio de Janeiro*

Contents

CHAPTER THREE

CHAPTER FOUR

CHAPTER FIVE

CHAPTER SIX

CHAPTER SEVEN

CHAPTER EIGHT

Preface

This is a book about how our national government makes economic policy. It was designed as a brief supplementary text to help students in introductory American government and public policy courses understand the political process.

I have described the interaction of major government institutions and the tools that they use to influence the nation's economy. The reader will soon realize that public policy decisions affect people in uneven ways. In short, there are winners and losers.

In preparing the text I have searched for a means of making policy-development understandable to students with diverse interests and backgrounds. Actual descriptions of recent decisions by the national government seem to me the most appropriate method of helping people to understand the ways in which economic policy is made. Therefore, I have included brief case studies of the Gramm-Rudman-Hollings Act, the 1981 tax reduction, the 1986 Tax Reform Act, the policies of the Federal Reserve System under Paul Volcker, the deregulation of the airline industry, the Chrysler bailout, and the United States–Canada Free-Trade Agreement.

This book assumes that most readers have a limited knowledge of economics. I have not attempted to write a highly theoretical or quantitative book. I doubt that I have the knowledge to do so, and, under any circumstances, my colleagues in political economy and economics have already written good texts and learned treatises for those who wish to know more about the intricacies of the economic system. My goal is more modest. If I succeed in helping undergraduates understand the ways in which governmental institutions make hard economic choices, that will be sufficient.

Like most authors, I have benefited from the assistance of others. I am particularly grateful to the reviewers, Lawrence W. O'Connell, University of New Hampshire; Mike R. Rubinoff, University of Pittsburgh, Greenburgh; and James F. Ward, University of Massachusetts, Boston, whose suggestions and criticisms helped to improve this book. My editor at Prentice Hall, Karen Horton, and her administrative assistant, Delores Mars, showed great patience and understanding as I wrote and revised the text. Three other people deserve special thanks. Michael Cecere and Joe Orosz provided valuable help by identifying bibliographical materials and proofreading parts of the book. Mari Bell-Nolan labored conscientiously in typing the manuscript. Her willingness to put up with my scrawls and changes in wording without complaint is greatly appreciated.

Whatever strengths this book exhibits are largely the result of the help I received from the persons I have mentioned and from others who work in various libraries and government offices. Any faults or weaknesses in the text are solely my responsibility.

Carl Lieberman
The University of Akron

CHAPTER ONE

Introduction

The government of the United States will spend over one-fifth of all the money generated by the American economy. Almost $350 billion is currently provided in Social Security and Medicare benefits. More than one-sixth of the funds allocated by state and local governments is derived from federal sources. Regulations concerning hiring practices, wages, working conditions, and the safety of goods and services will be published and enforced by thousands of civil servants. The supply of money will be significantly affected by a banking system created by Congress in the early years of this century. In short, every major aspect of the American economic system is influenced by the policies of the national government.

In order to explain the intricate workings of federal economic policy, it is necessary to understand the tools that the national government has at its disposal, as well as the actors who are involved in decision-making. This chapter examines both of these topics and suggests some alternative ways of understanding how economic policy is made.

THE ECONOMIC TOOLS OF THE FEDERAL GOVERNMENT

The United States government has five major tools at its disposal in making economic policy: taxation, spending, regulation of the money supply, industrial and commercial regulation, and economic subsidies. Although these tools are sometimes viewed as separate components in making economic policy, they are actually interrelated.

Fiscal policy—taxation and spending—is perhaps the most vital aspect of federal economic decision-making. In fiscal year 1991, the expenditures of the U.S. government will exceed $1.2 trillion. That amount is equivalent to nearly 22 percent of the *gross national product* (GNP), which is the value of all goods and services produced in our country. As a result of the gap between expenditures and revenues, the federal debt grew during fiscal year 1990 by almost $200 billion.[1]

Spending and taxing are important not only because they affect the total patterns of consumption in the United States, but also because they reflect the priorities of the national government. For example, during the last 20 years, spending has shifted so that social welfare, rather than defense, has become the largest area of federal expenditure. Similarly, when Congress and the president have wanted businesses to engage in certain behaviors—more investment or greater pension benefits for employees—the tax code has been adjusted to provide incentives for acting accordingly.

The regulation of the money supply—monetary policy—refers to the processes by which government controls and adjusts the amount of funds available for loans and economic expansion. As we will note in a later chapter, the Federal Reserve System plays a particularly crucial role in expanding or contracting the money supply.[2]

Economic regulation is vital in a society in which national and multinational corporations are major actors, 90 percent of the labor force is employed by others, the marketplace is generally impersonal, and products are not subject to close scrutiny by the consumer. To a significant degree, the executive departments, including Commerce, Agriculture, Labor, and Justice, are responsible for implementing programs of regulation. However, the independent regulatory commissions are more directly involved in controlling major areas of the economy. Thus, the Federal Communications Commission issues licenses to radio and television stations and sets rates for interstate telephone calls, while the Federal Trade Commission has the power to forbid unfair trade practices.[3]

Economic subsidies can be defined broadly to include all forms of welfare and financial transfers. However, as the term is used in this book, it refers to direct or indirect assistance designed to help certain industries, make workers more productive, or give certain individuals and businesses a competitive edge over others. Training programs for workers, mortgage insurance for the housing industry, and low-interest loans to farmers and businesspeople are among the programs encompassed by subsidies.

As we examine the tools available to governmental decision-makers, it is important to recognize a simple but sometimes overlooked fact: Public policies often serve more than one purpose. A minimum wage is a regulatory policy that compels employers to pay a minimum amount fixed by law to those who work for them. However, it is also an indirect subsidy, which provides some workers a slightly higher wage than they would otherwise receive and helps those who earn more than that minimum hourly rate to bargain for additional income whenever it is raised. Tariffs are taxes on imported goods. They also perform a regulatory function because they effectively restrict the goods that consumers can purchase by raising their price. In addition, tariffs aid some domestic producers by reducing the ability of producers of foreign goods to compete with U.S. producers. The mixed functions of economic policies is a significant feature that can assist us in understanding the complex consequences of government decisions.

THE ACTORS INVOLVED IN MAKING ECONOMIC POLICY

It is difficult to summarize briefly the actors involved in making national economic policy. Nevertheless, as Figure 1–1 suggests, economic policy-making involves actors within and outside the federal government. All branches of the government participate in decision-making.

Economic policy-making can be thought of as occurring within a system composed of the activities of a number of interrelated actors. **Inputs** refer to the demands made to alter economic policy; those demands are made mainly by interest groups, including major business and labor organizations. Demands are directed to government decision-makers. Government responds to the demands of interest groups by making public policy. These policy **outputs** lead to certain **outcomes**, benefiting or rewarding some segments of society while imposing costs or penalties on others. The process is never completed, for as decisions are made, groups are affected differently. Those harmed by a policy will communicate with government

Figure 1–1 Actors involved in economic policy-making.

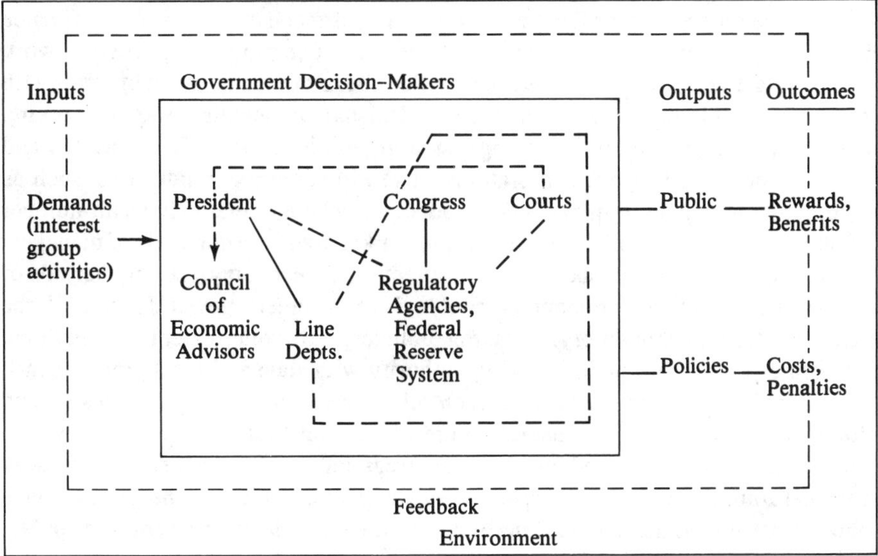

officials and urge the policy's modification or repeal. This process of constant communication between the governed and those who make policy is known as **feedback**. All policy-making takes place in a broader economic, social, and political environment.[4]

Government decision-makers influence economic policy in various ways. The Council of Economic Advisers advises the president on economic policy and assists him in the preparation of his annual economic message to Congress. The president and Congress make broad policies concerning taxation, spending, regulation, and subsidies. The line departments, which are charged with carrying out governmental policy—Labor, Commerce, Justice, and so on—are legally responsible to the president. Although their primary function is to carry out the policies of Congress and the president, they also make proposals and assess the feasibility of policy alternatives. The chief function of the Federal Reserve System is to regulate the money supply. The regulatory agencies have been created by Congress to exercise control over selected areas of the economy. They have the power to make rules, conduct hearings, and impose penalties. The actions of regulatory agencies can be reviewed by the judiciary, as can the policies of other government bodies. The courts may ultimately invalidate laws or executive actions if they are found to be unconstitutional.

Major elected officials—the president and members of Congress—operate in an atmosphere that is often politically charged. The nature of their positions makes them visible to the press and thus to the news-following public. As officeholders, they are also accessible to many political activists, organized groups, and government "insiders" (bureaucrats, judges, and other officials). It is little wonder, then, that the decisions they make are likely to be influenced by the pressures that are exerted upon them by other actors in the political process.

The environment in which economic policy is made is one in which influence is generally dispersed. Approximately 85 percent of employed U.S. citizens work in the private sector, and most members of the labor force are engaged by firms with fewer than 100 employees. Thus, most decisions concerning wages, working conditions,and production are being made in millions of small businesses and farms, rather than in giant corporations. Even in certain key industries, such as automobile manufacturing and steel production, where a relatively small number of major companies dominate the domestic market, there are hundreds of managers and union officials who make decisions affecting the economy. During periods of peace, the federal government is rarely given complete power to control the economy through regulatory or taxing policies. To some extent, the national authorities must share policy-making authority with state and local governments, which traditionally have exercised control over many aspects of industry and commerce. Therefore, the federal nature of our constitutional system, in which government power is shared by central and regional decision-makers, discourages national domination.[5] Moreover, the American political culture—the ideas we have about what government should do and how it should do it—prevent total public control of the economy.[6]

UNDERSTANDING HOW ECONOMIC POLICY IS MADE

Given the number of actors involved and the many policies formulated and implemented by the national government, there can be no simple explanation of how economic policy is made. Nevertheless, there are several models that can assist us in understanding the factors that lead to specific economic decisions. We must begin our examination of economic policy-making by recognizing that many routine policies are devised by a limited group of actors. Although the president and Congress must necessarily be involved in the passage of legislation, three groups—bureaucratic agencies, the interests served by these bureaucratic bodies, and the congressional committees or subcommittees—decide the form that many bills will take. As Figure 1–2 suggests, these sets of actors can be viewed as sharing a triangular relationship. Indeed, some students of American government have referred to this relationship as the "iron triangle."[7]

It is not surprising that the president and most members of Congress are only tangentially concerned with many of the policies made by the national government. Most of the legislation considered by the House and the Senate, as well as the rules made by executive departments or regulatory agencies, affect a relatively small segment of the American people. For example, price supports for dairy products and regulations for migrant farm workers are of great importance to those concerned, and they may even have significant long-range effects on the prices we pay for certain foods. However, their direct impact on most of the population is negligible. Moreover, many of the changes embodied in these policies are not very controversial. If they do not arouse much opposition, they are not likely to be covered extensively by the media. Thus, they can be handled by the less visible process of negotiations among the three sets of actors who have been described.

In a sense, the iron triangle represents a process by which interest groups communicate their concerns and demands to relevant decision-makers in the government.

Not everyone accepts the notion that the iron triangle, or "subgovernments," control the major aspects of policy-making. Some analysts argue that **issue net-**

Figure 1–2 The iron triangle.

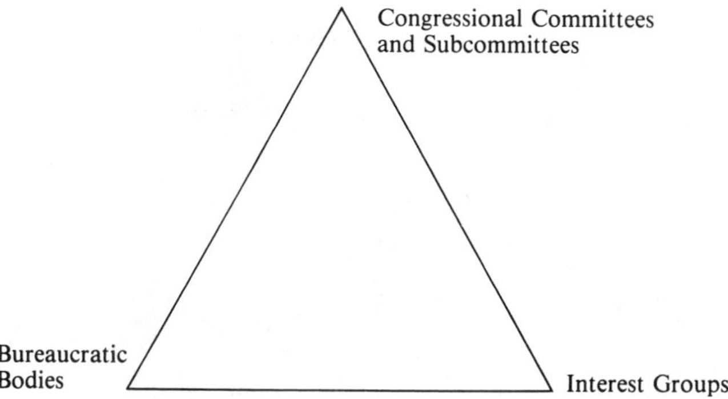

works, consisting of public officials, interest-group representatives, political activists, technical and policy experts, research organizations, and the like, often focus on a specific concern. These groups move in and out of the network and are motivated by ideas and beliefs concerning public policy as well as by material considerations.[8] When we examine airline deregulation, we will find that the concept of issue networks is helpful in understanding the decisions that were made.

Although the motivations of those involved in economic policy-making are complex, most scholars would probably agree that perceived self-interest plays a significant part in determining why people behave as they do. Of course, behavior cannot be understood only in individual terms. The interests of people are usually represented by organized groups that lobby in their behalf. Some have argued that government largely responds to organized pressure groups, making policy in accordance with the wishes of the most powerful interests. This "group theory" of politics sees government institutions essentially as puppets, whose strings are pulled by powerful external forces (see Figure 1–3).[9]

Organized interests unquestionably play an important role in making economic policy. Business, labor, and agricultural organizations all try to influence executive, legislative, and judicial officials. These groups typically voice their opinions concerning spending, taxing, regulatory, and subsidy policies. Sometimes they testify before congressional committees, while on other occasions they lobby relevant executive officers or take action to halt the implementation of programs through court action. However, to note that interest groups participate in making policy is not to say that

Figure 1–3 Government as as agent of interest-group pressure.

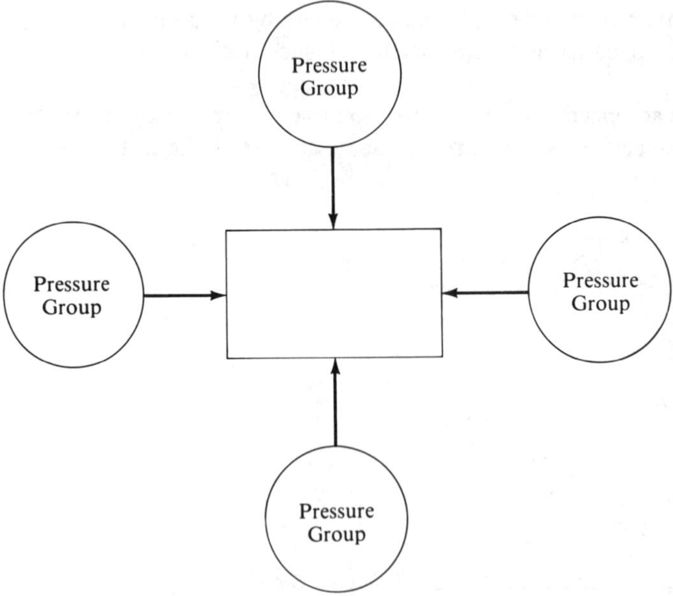

they simply direct government action. Not all interest groups have the ability to secure access—a place in the political process where one's voice can be heard and one's views can be seriously considered. Furthermore, interest groups do not always initiate policy; they are occasionally mobilized by government officials who seek their support in behalf of additional appropriations or programmatic change.

One way to explain why some groups and individuals are more successful than others in achieving their objectives is to examine the resources that they possess. If we consider the making of public policy a form of transaction by which material benefits or symbolic rewards can be allocated, then we may ask how those outside the government can influence this allocation. Individuals or groups can exchange support and political favors (e.g., campaign contributions, votes, endorsements, information) for public policies that they favor (Figure 1–4). Those individuals and groups with greater resources—more money, greater prestige, and the like—can trade with government officials in order to receive more access and greater success in achieving policy goals.[10]

ALTERNATIVE DIRECTIONS FOR THE ECONOMY

The directions that government can take in influencing the economy are as important as the actors involved in making economic policy. Broadly speaking, there are two forms of ownership of the means of production and exchange. Public or government ownership is characteristic of socialist systems, while private ownership is typical of capitalist economies.

In practice, however, there are few if any "pure" or ideal economic systems. The Soviet Union, for example, permits limited forms of private and cooperative ownership. Democratic socialist governments in Western Europe do not advocate the abolition of all private property and production. And although the United States is often described as a capitalist society, it has important elements of public ownership and operation. The public schools, the postal service, and some utilities are among the government owned enterprises in our country. Thus, we have a mixed economic system, composed of important elements of public and private ownership.[11]

Mixed economies, such as those found in the United States and other western nations, usually provide for a wide array of public rules affecting consumer safety,

Figure 1–4 Policy-making as a form of political exchange.

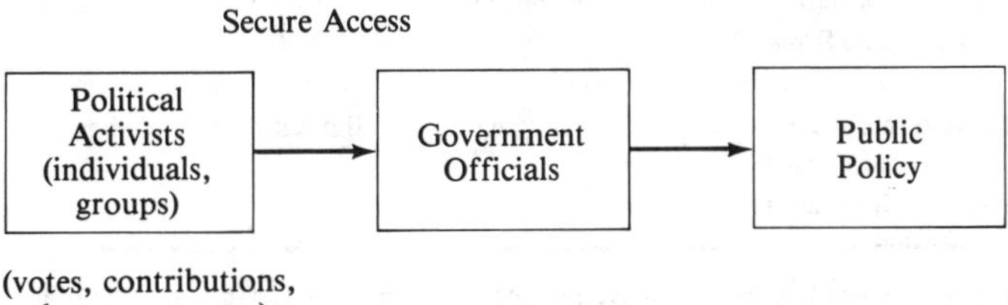

working conditions, marketing of products, and the like. Government also comes to the aid of businesses, farmers, and workers through various forms of subsidies and tax incentives.

Mixed economies recognize the importance of market forces—competition, risk-taking, entrepreneurship, bargaining over wages and prices—but they also provide an important role for public intervention. An underlying assumption of advocates of government regulation and aid is that the market operates imperfectly to allocate needed goods and services or to reward people adequately for their labor. Moreover, some fear that, if left to their own devices, business owners would conspire to fix prices and reduce competition, thus defeating the very purpose of a free market.[12]

Opponents of government intervention in the economy generally believe that the market is more capable than the government of making decisions about production, marketing, and pricing. They contend that government, which is not motivated by a desire for profit or greater value for monies expended, is unlikely to allocate resources wisely. They may also be fearful of granting excessive power to public officials. Advocates of free-market economics are likely to see individual control over property as among the more important rights that people possess.

The major conflict between politicians and activists over government intervention in our nation's enconomy, however, is not between proponents of socialism on the one hand and those who support a laissez faire system, devoid of state involvement, on the other. Rather, it is between those who want a greater or smaller role for the public sector in making decisions of an economic nature.

Political considerations, of course, affect the actual decisions that government officials make when a controversial question arises. Thus, a serious drought, such as the one that occurred in the summer of 1988, will lead a president and members

Advocates of a Major Role for Government	Advocates of a Limited Role for Government
Favor some forms of public ownership (e.g., electrical generating facilities, such as dams and power plants; public housing for low-income people; industries involved in developing new forms of energy, etc.).	Favor elimination or reduction of government owned facilities. Tend to support "privatization" of publicly owned facilities.
Favor greater government regulation to protect workers, consumers, the environment, etc. In some cases, favor higher tariffs or quotas on imported goods to assist American firms.	Favor deregulation or simplified regulations. Usually advocate free trade or the reduction of trade barriers.
Favor subsidies for workers and industries in need, particularly those adversely affected by foreign competition or economic dislocation.	Favor reduction or elimination of subsidies.

Figure 1–5 Differences in the views of advocates of greater and lesser government intervention in the economy.

of Congress who generally favor a limited role for government in the economy to support substantial economic aid for farmers. Congresspeople whose districts include an industry that is meeting substantial competition from imported goods may favor trade restrictions on those products, regardless of their general opposition to government "meddling" in the economy.

SUMMARY

We have described several tools that the federal government uses to influence the economy: taxation, spending, regulation of the money supply, industrial and commercial regulation, and subsidies. The role of interest groups and government institutions has also been discussed. We have noted that the environment affects the extent and nature of public intervention in the economy. Organized groups can often exert influence on government decision-makers. Many policies are made by the interaction of interest groups, congressional committees, and bureaucratic agencies. Individuals and groups who wish to gain access to government and achieve their goals may do so through various forms of political exchange. Issue networks also explain the multitude of actors involved in certain decisions and their complex motivations.

There are two general directions in which public decision-makers can move. The first provides for greater government intervention in the economy, whether through more government ownership, regulation, or subsidies. The second favors greater reliance on the marketplace and a reduction in the role of the public sector.

In the chapters that follow, we will examine in greater detail how the national government employs fiscal, monetary, regulatory, and subsidy policies. We will consider actual cases in which controversial policies were made, and we will examine what these instances of decision-making tell us about the American political process.

NOTES

[1]At the beginning of 1990, the Office of Management and Budget was estimating a deficit for fiscal 1990 of $123.8 billion. See Executive Office of the President, Office of Management and Budget, *The Budget for Fiscal Year 1991* (Washington, D.C.: 1990), p. 2. As a result of the cost of the savings and loan "bailout" and slow economic growth, the Congressional Budget Office in July, 1990 estimated a $200 billion shortfall for fiscal 1990. See Congress of the United States, Congressional Budget Office, *The Economic and Budget Outlook: An Update* (Washington, DC: Congressional Budget Office, 1990), pp. ix-xi.

[2]For a general discussion of the operations of the Federal Reserve System, see Michael D. Reagan, "The Political Structure of the Federal Reserve System," *The American Political Science Review*, 55 (March 1961), 64–76; and Thibaut de Saint Phalle, *The Federal Reserve: An Intentional Mystery* (New York: Praeger, 1985).

[3]The functions of the independent regulatory commissions are described by Peter Woll, *American Bureaucracy* (2d ed.; New York: W. W. Norton & Co., Inc., 1977); and by Louis M. Kohlmeier, Jr., *The Regulators* (New York: Harper & Row, Pub., 1969).

[4]The systems approach is dealt with by David Easton in *The Political System: An Inquiry into the State of Political Science* (2d ed., New York: Alfred A. Knopf, 1971), particularly pp. 96–100; and in *A Systems Analysis of Political Life* (New York: John Wiley, 1965).

[5]Daniel J. Elazar, *American Federalism: A View from the States* (3d ed.; New York: Harper & Row, Pub., 1984), particularly Chapters 1 and 2.

[6]Although government action is bound to help some people more than others, an economic system based primarily upon private ownership discourages overall governmental planning and frequent public intervention. Privatism dominated the economic development of the United States. See Sam Bass Warner, Jr., *The Private City: Philadelphia in Three Periods of Its Growth* (Philadelphia: University of Pennsylvania Press, 1968). Also see the remarks of Daniel Elazar concerning the individualistic political culture (Elazar, p. 115).

[7]The term *subsystem* or *subgovernment* is sometimes applied to the bureaucrats, interest groups, and members of congressional subcommittees involved in a limited area of public policy. See A. Lee Fritschler, *Smoking and Politics: Policymaking and the Federal Bureaucracy* (New York: Meredith, 1969), pp. 2–5, 8–9; James E. Anderson, *Public Policy-Making* (New York: Praeger, 1975), pp. 50–51; and Randall B. Ripley and Grace A. Franklin, *Congress; the Bureaucracy; and Public Policy* (3d ed.; Homewood, IL: Dorsey Press, 1984), pp. 8–12.

[8]James E. Anderson, *Public Policymaking: An Introduction* (Boston: Houghton Mifflin, 1990), p. 71.

[9]For a discussion of interest groups and the group theory of politics, see Arthur Fisher Bentley, *The Process of Government: A Study of Social Pressures* (Bloomington, IN: Principia Press, 1935); Earl Latham, *The Group Basis of Politics: A Study in Basing-Point Legislation* (New York: Octagon, 1965); and David B. Truman, *The Governmental Process: Political Interests and Public Opinion* (2d ed.; New York: Knopf, 1971).

[10]For a useful examination of how exchange theory operates, see Robert J. Sickels, *Presidential Transactions* (Englewood Cliffs, NJ: Prentice Hall, 1974). Also, see Thomas A. Reilly and Michael W. Sigall, *Political Bargaining: An Introduction to Modern Politics* (San Francisco: W. H. Freeman & Company Publishers, 1976).

[11]William N. Loucks, *Comparative Economic Systems* (7th ed.; New York: Harper & Row, Pub., 1965), pp. 19–41 and 199–229. See also William Ebenstein, *Today's Isms* (7th ed.; Englewood Cliffs, NJ: Prentice Hall, 1973), pp. 139–259, for a discussion of the political implications of capitalism and socialism.

[12]As Adam Smith, the leading proponent of classical capitalism, noted in *The Wealth of Nations*, "People of the same trade seldom meet together but the conversation ends in a conspiracy against the public, or in some diversion to raise prices." Cited in Robert L. Heilbroner, *The Worldly Philosophers: The Lives, Times, and Ideas of the Great Economic Thinkers* (6th ed.; New York: Simon & Schuster, 1986), p. 70.

CHAPTER TWO

Fiscal Policy: An Introduction

The major objectives of economic policy are to stabilize the economy at high employment, maintain price stability, and promote growth and efficiency.[1]

Joseph Pechman

THE CHANGING NATURE OF FISCAL POLICY

There are two major ways in which the federal government can try to influence such macroeconomic factors as overall growth of the economy, employment, and rate of inflation. It can seek to control (1) the supply of money or (2) the level of spending and taxation. Decisions about expenditures and taxes are the components of fiscal policy.

Historically, Democrats have been more inclined to use fiscal policy, while Republicans tend to emphasize monetary policy in pursuing major economic goals.[2] The assumptions of fiscal policy-makers have changed over the years.

For approximately the first 150 years of our history as an independent country, federal budget policy rested on the notion that annual receipts and expenditures should roughly match each other. When there was a recession, it was necessary to raise taxes or reduce spending.

By the 1930s, the ideas of John Maynard Keynes, the British economist, became more prominent. This new view of fiscal policy held that higher taxes and lower government expenditures were useful in fighting inflation, while lower taxes and higher expenditures would help combat recession. Balanced budgets each year were no longer thought necessary.

More recently, economists and public officials have come to see fiscal policy as only one important tool to stimulate or check the economy. The supply of money and credit is also viewed as a major means of affecting growth and stability.[3] The economic stagnation and relatively high inflation rates that we suffered during the middle to late 1970s led many people to question the value of taxation and spending as means of significantly improving economic prospects.

FISCAL POLICY-MAKERS

Many actors are involved in the fiscal policy-making process. Although we will discuss their roles at greater length in the chapters on taxation and spending policy, a brief description of the functions they perform follows.

Among the most important decision-makers are the president, the Office of Management and Budget (OMB), the secretary of the Treasury, the Congressional Budget Office, the budget committees of the House and Senate, the Senate Finance Committee, the House Ways and Means Committee, and the appropriations committees of both chambers of Congress.

The president is responsible by law for submitting an executive budget to Congress each year, showing anticipated revenues and outlays. The presidential budget provides an opportunity to set priorities and maintain some control over the bureaucracy.

The Office of Management and Budget negotiates with executive departments and agencies and tries to operate within the guidelines established by the president in preparing the budget. The OMB also enforces budgetary cuts authorized by the president.

The secretary of the Treasury heads the department responsible for collecting taxes and managing the public debt. He is likely to be consulted before major proposals are sent to Congress on taxation or expenditures.

The Congressional Budget Office (CBO) advises the House and Senate budget committees. It provides its own estimates concerning the revenues, outlays, and deficits in the forthcoming fiscal year. The budget committees in turn recommend to their respective houses the amount to be spent by the federal government, including the sums to be allocated for major public purposes. Thus, some broad boundaries can be established on the level and nature of federal spending.

The Senate Finance Committee and the House Ways and Means Committee are the congressional committees that review tax legislation before it goes to the floor of their respective chambers for a vote. These committees play a major role in deciding the detailed provisions of changes in the tax code.

Before monies can be allocated for a new or existing program of the federal government, they must be authorized by a substantive standing committee of each house (e.g., the House Labor and Education Committee or the Senate Armed Services Committee). However, before funds are actually given to a department or agency of the government for the following fiscal year, they must be appropriated by Congress. The House and Senate committees on appropriations thus have substantial power to affect the sums of money available for programmatic purposes and the conditions under which they can be used.[4]

Without even considering the role of interest groups and prominent constituents who influence taxing and spending, we see that there are many governmental actors who affect fiscal policy. They represent different entities within the national government and are likely to defend the powers and prerogatives of these bodies, as well as the concerns of the specific groups with which they are aligned.

SUMMARY

The two most important means for influencing major economic forces in our country are monetary policy and fiscal policy. We have noted that in recent years skepticism has increased concerning the ability of fiscal policy to stabilize the economy.

There are numerous fiscal policy-makers in both the executive and legislative branches of government. Each body of decision-makers has its own base of power, political support, and expertise.

In the chapters that follow we will consider at greater length spending and tax policies. We will examine the budgetary process, varying perspectives on federal spending, and deficit reductions. We will also discuss issues involved in tax policy, as well as the 1981 tax reduction and the 1986 Tax Reform Act.

NOTES

[1]Joseph Pechman, *Federal Tax Policy* (5th ed.; Washington, DC: The Brookings Institution, 1987), p. 9.

[2]Paul Peretz, "The Politics of Fiscal and Monetary Policy," in *The Politics of American Economic Policy Making*, ed. Paul Peretz (Armonk, NY: M. E. Sharpe, 1987), p. 140.

[3]Pechman, p. 8.

[4]For a discussion of the budget and the congressional role in allocating funds, see Aaron Wildavsky, *The Politics of the Budgetary Process* (4th ed.; Boston: Little, Brown, 1984).

CHAPTER THREE

Spending Policy

> As quickly as you start spending federal money in large amounts, it looks like free money.[1]
>
> *Dwight D. Eisenhower*

> The Federal Government is the people and the budget is a reflection of their need.[2]
>
> *John F. Kennedy*

THE FEDERAL BUDGETARY PROCESS

Presidents Eisenhower and Kennedy expressed two different views of the federal budget. Eisenhower emphasized the tendency of the national government to spend in an uninhibited and even profligate manner. His successor saw federal expenditures in a more generous light, focusing on the way in which they meet popular needs.

Both chief executives were partly correct. It is easy for public officials and the groups that make demands on the political system to view government expenditures for particular programs as endless and without limit. Nevertheless, the budget is ultimately a compendium of social needs and desires, as mediated by the president, government agencies, congressional committees, and interest groups.

If we are to understand how decisions are made to allocate federal monies, we must consider who is involved in budget-making and the kinds of pressures they encounter. The budgetary process is complex, involving a multitude of actors within and outside the government.

Until 1921, there was not a single budget document submitted by the executive branch to Congress. Federal departments and agencies merely presented their individual requests to the appropriations committees of each house (see Figure 3–1). The process was highly fragmented and effectively prevented any centralized control over the expenditure of public funds.[3]

In 1921 the Budget and Accounting Act was signed into law. It created the Bureau of the Budget, which was originally in the Treasury Department, to assist the

Figure 3–1 House Appropriations Committee.

president in preparing a budget. The budget would recommend allocations to various federal agencies and departments and estimate the revenues that the national government would receive in the forthcoming fiscal year. The president was responsible for presenting an annual budget to Congress at the beginning of each calendar year.[4]

The Bureau of the Budget was transferred to the Executive Office of the President in the administration of Franklin Roosevelt.[5] It was renamed the Office of Management and Budget (OMB) during the Nixon administration, and it has several responsibilities in addition to preparing a budget. It clears and coordinates legislation for the president, promotes managerial improvement within the executive branch, and checks the implementation of presidential programs to promote economy and efficiency.[6]

The passage and implementation of the Congressional Budget and Impoundment Control Act of 1974 created budget committees in each house of Congress and gave them a detailed calendar to set guidelines for federal expenditures (see Figure 3–2). The Congressional Budget Office (CBO) was established, and it was assigned the task of estimating the cost of proposed legislation so that legislators could make more rational fiscal decisions.[7] In order to give Congress more time to make budgetary policy, the start of the fiscal year was changed from July 1 to October 1.[8]

The creation of a new budgetary calendar and a different structure for making decisions altered, but did not eliminate, the existing budgetary process. Many of the actors who had made spending and taxing policy continued to play prominent roles.

First Monday after January 3
President submits executive budget

February 15
CBO reports to budget committees on fiscal policy and budget priorities

February 25
Congressional Committees submit reports and estimates to budget committees

April 1
Senate Budget Committee reports budget resolution to floor

April 15
Congress completes action on budget resolution

June 10
House Appropriations Committee reports last regular appropriations bill

June 15
Congress completes action on reconciliation bill

June 30
House completes action on regular appropriations bills

August 15
OMB and CBO estimate budget deficit. President reports whether he intends to take steps to protect military personnel and other accounts if automatic cuts are ordered.

August 25
Director of OMB submits report to president and Congress on estimated deficit for following fiscal year and amount of deficit reduction that has resulted from laws enacted and regulations promulgated

October 1
Fiscal year begins

October 15
Director of OMB submits revised report on estimated deficits; initial and revised reports become basis for sequester orders by president if they are necessary to reduce deficits

---

*Calendar has been revised by the Balanced Budget and Emergency Deficit Control Act of 1985 (Gramm-Rudman-Hollings Act).

Source: *Congressional Quarterly Weekly Report* (December 14, 1985), p. 2608; and Executive Office of the President, Office of Management and Budget, *The United States Budget in Brief, Fiscal Year 1989* (Washington, DC: U.S. Government Printing Office, 1988) pp. 94–95.

Figure 3–2 Congressional budget process timetable.*

Spending programs still had to be authorized by committees with oversight responsibilities for the various executive departments and agencies. Specific sums to be appropriated for the forthcoming fiscal year would first be approved by the

House and Senate appropriations committees. Tax bills to pay for federal expenditures must be submitted to the House Ways and Means and Senate Finance Committees.

If prominent legislative actors continue to play important roles in making budgetary decisions, it is no less true that the pressures that they face remain largely the same. Powerful interest groups and some individual citizens ask for federal money to pay for programs they believe should be publicly supported. Most groups, whether business-oriented or not, prefer to shift the costs of federal expenditures to others, rather than accepting the full burden of added taxation. We want a more generous and responsive government to meet the multitude of social needs that we perceive, but we also feel overtaxed and unwilling to accept the cost of additional spending.

A second and perhaps even more immediate problem that members of Congress face is how to make practical decisions concerning the allocation of monies to the many bodies and programs that are funded by the national government. Over the years a number of ideas have been proposed, and some have been adopted in part by federal budget-makers.

For example, a program-planning budget (PPB) system to match expenditures with broad programmatic goals was tried by the Johnson administration.[9] Zero-base budgeting (ZBB) was proposed and partially implemented by the Carter administration in its early years in office. This budgetary system, which is used in some American states, requires a thorough justification of all programmatic expenditures by governmental agencies, either on an annual or other periodic basis. Presumably no expenditures are to be taken for granted; in that sense, the budget starts from a base of zero dollars.[10]

Although each of these means of controlling expenditures has its supporters and critics, neither provides a sure-fire method of helping members of Congress decide on the amounts needed by the government for the following fiscal year. In truth, members of the House and Senate probably use a variety of "decision rules" when voting on appropriations measures. Most are likely to rely on the recommendations of their colleagues on the budget and appropriations committees, because they are seen as having more knowledge concerning policies on expenditures.[11] In some cases they vote for bills that they know will benefit their constituents (e.g., for a new dam or a defense contract likely to be awarded to a firm in their district or state). **Log-rolling**, whereby a legislator agrees to vote for a measure dear to another member's constituents in return for his or her support for a similar bill affecting those the legislator represents, is another way of making economic decisions.[12]

According to scholars who have studied the budgetary process, one of the most common rules of thumb in deciding what to allocate to which federal agencies is to provide slightly more than what was given the year before. This process of gradually increasing expenditures, known as **incrementalism**, has certain advantages. It is relatively easy to understand, and it usually involves fewer political costs than other methods one might try to apply. After all, thorough reexaminations of existing programs are time-consuming and could lead to political repercussions if popular ones are gutted as a result of the review process.[13] How many people would wish to examine Social Security anew every few years? Who would want to look closely at the multitude of defense expenditures that are made annually? Even most detractors of governmental spending don't seriously question the need for the majority of programs currently in place.

In recent years, as deficits have grown and an administration has been in power that wanted to cut taxes, reduce social welfare expenditures, and allocate additional sums to the military, it has become necessary for legislators to confront the unpleasant task of making some reductions in federal spending. Thus, instead of a simple incremental model, Congress has turned in some cases to **decrementalism**, the process of making gradual or moderate cuts in existing programs.[14] Occasionally, legislators have even eliminated some areas of expenditure, as they did when they voted in 1986 to abolish general revenue sharing, a system of allocating funds for nonspecified purposes to state and local governments.[15]

What one must remember about both incremental and decremental spending is that they give decision-makers, particularly generalists or "nonexperts," an opportunity to make allocations fairly quickly and without much controversy. Moreover, they allow elected officials to resist some of the pressures that are imposed upon them by groups seeking more aid from the public coffers. One can always argue that an incremental process provides a little more for most programs. Under a decremental pattern, many agencies or programs are likely to have suffered cutbacks; thus, many groups have had to share the hardships of austerity.

Of course, neither incrementalism nor decrementalism is without its critics. Both processes avoid a thorough examination of how money is spent and whether stated objectives are actually being accomplished. Incrementalism works best when revenues are steadily increasing and deficit spending is not seen as a major problem. It accepts the growth of government and fails to challenge the need for additional allocation of public resources.

Decrementalism tends to apply cuts broadly but often fails to establish clear-cut priorities for reducing expenditures. Moreover, in a period of decremental spending, powerful political forces are likely to seek exemptions from proposed reductions for their preferred agencies or programs, or they may try to shift the burden of these cuts to others. As we will see, there are several ways in which clever actors can hide the size of deficits and avoid the full force of budget slashes.

THE BUDGET AS A POLITICAL DOCUMENT

To understand the process of budget-making, we must recognize that the federal budget is a political document. The president's recommendations for expenditures represent his administration's priorities as well as its response to the demands of various groups for new programs or altered funding.

Over the last three decades the fiscal preferences of the United States government have changed. A higher proportion of public monies are now allocated to interest payments on the national debt and social welfare expenditures (most of which are benefit payments to individuals) than was the case in the 1960s (Tables 3–1 and 3–2 and Figures 3–3, 3–4).

TABLE 3–1 Composition of Budget Outlays in Current Prices: 1963–1994 (in billions of dollars)

NONDEFENSE

Fiscal Year	Total Outlays	National Defense	Total Nondefense	Payments for Individuals	Net Interest	All Other
1963	111.3	50.1	61.2	30.4	7.7	23.1
1964	118.6	51.5	67.1	31.6	8.2	27.3
1965	118.4	47.5	71.0	32.3	8.6	30.1
1966	134.7	54.9	79.8	36.2	9.4	34.2
1967	157.6	68.2	89.4	43.1	10.3	36.0
1968	178.1	78.8	99.4	48.7	11.1	39.6
1969	183.6	79.4	104.2	55.3	12.7	36.3
1970	195.7	78.6	117.1	63.2	14.4	39.6
1971	210.2	75.8	134.4	78.7	14.8	40.9
1972	230.7	76.6	154.1	90.8	15.5	47.9
1973	245.6	74.5	171.1	102.1	17.3	51.6
1974	267.9	77.8	190.1	117.5	21.4	51.2
1975	324.2	85.6	238.7	150.4	23.2	65.1
1976	364.5	89.4	275.0	176.6	26.7	71.7
1977	400.5	97.5	303.0	192.4	29.9	80.8
1978	448.4	105.2	343.2	206.5	35.4	101.3
1979	491.0	117.7	373.3	227.5	42.6	103.2
1980	576.7	135.9	440.8	271.1	62.5	117.2
1981	657.2	159.8	497.4	316.6	68.7	112.1
1982	728.4	187.4	541.0	348.6	84.7	107.7
1983	808.3	209.9	598.4	395.4	89.8	103.2
1984	851.8	227.4	624.4	398.8	111.1	114.5
1985	946.3	252.7	693.6	425.6	129.4	138.6
1986	990.3	273.4	716.9	449.4	136.0	131.5
1987	1,003.8	282.0	721.8	469.4	138.6	113.8
1988	1,064.0	290.4	773.7	498.8	151.7	123.2
1989	1,142.6	303.6	839.0	534.5	169.1	135.4
1990 estimate	1,197.2	296.3	900.9	564.5	175.6	160.8
1991 estimate	1,233.3	303.3	930.0	603.4	173.0	153.6
1992 estimate	1,271.4	309.2	962.2	643.4	163.5	155.3
1993 estimate	1,327.6	311.9	1,015.7	680.1	157.0	178.6
1994 estimate	1,408.6	315.7	1,092.9	718.1	147.8	227.0

Note: For fiscal years 1975–1994, includes off-budget amounts.

Source: Executive Office of the President, Office of Management and Budget, *The United States Budget in Brief, Fiscal Year 1984* (Washington, DC: U.S. Government Printing Office, 1983) and *Fiscal Year 1990* (Washington, DC: U.S. Government Printing Office, 1989); and *Budget of the United States Government Fiscal Year 1991* (Washington, DC: U.S. Government Printing Office, 1990).

TABLE 3–2 Summary of Budget Expenditures and Deficits, Fiscal 1986–1993 (in billions of dollars)

	1986	1987	1988	1989	1990*	1991*	1992*	1993*
Receipts	769.1	854.1	909.0	990.7	1,073.5	1,170.2	1,246.4	1,327.6
Outlays	989.8	1,004.6	1,064.0	1,142.7	1,197.2	1,233.3	1,271.4	1,321.8
Surplus or deficit (-)	-220.7	-150.4	-155.1	-152.0	-123.8	-63.1	-25.1	-5.7
Gramm-Rudman-Hollings deficit targets	-171.9	-144.0	-144.0	-136.0	-100.0	-64.0	-28.0	0.0
Difference	48.8	6.4	11.1	16.0	23.8	-0.9	-2.9	-5.7

*Estimates.

Source: Executive Office of the President, Office of Management and Budget, *Budget of the United States Government, Fiscal Year 1988* (Washington, DC: U.S. Government Printing Office, 1987), p. 2–2; *The United States Budget in Brief, Fiscal Year 1990* (Washington, DC: U.S. Government Printing Office, 1989), p. 4; and *Budget of the United States Government, Fiscal Year 1991* (Washington, DC: U.S. Government Printing Office, 1990), p. A281.

Figure 3–3 Federal government outlays as percentages of GNP.

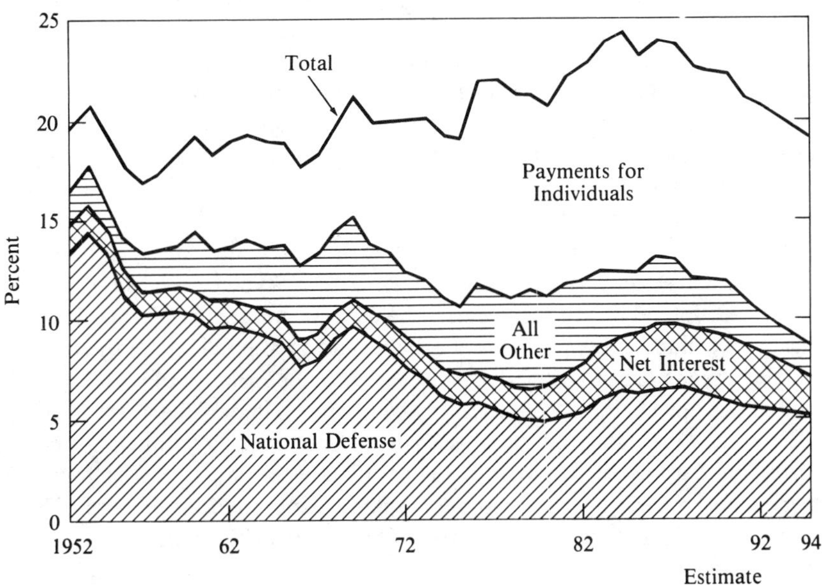

Source: Executive Office of the President, Office of Management and Budget, *Historical Tables: Budget of the United States Government, Fiscal Year 1990* (Washington, DC: U.S. Government Printing Office, 1989).

The Federal Government Dollar
Fiscal Year 1991 Estimate

Where It Comes From. . .

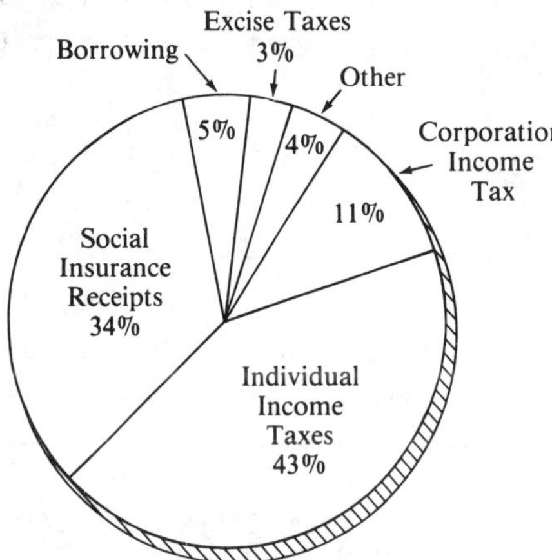

Where It Goes. . .

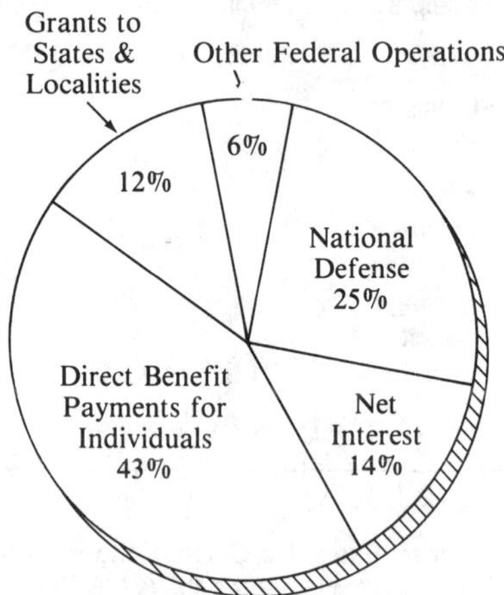

Source: Executive Office of the President, Office of Management and Budget, *Budget of the United States Government, Fiscal Year 1991* (Washington, DC: U.S. Government Printing Office, 1990), p. 2.

Figure 3–4 Source and distribution of federal revenues, 1991.

A determined and ideologically committed chief executive can bring about changes in patterns of federal expenditures. Thus, when Ronald Reagan was elected to the presidency, he began a policy of rapid increases in military spending and decreased emphasis on funding for housing, food stamps, and public assistance. Social welfare programs for the poor underwent the most severe cuts, although Congress modified some of the administration's proposals.[16]

Both the executive and legislative branches, however, are limited in the extent to which they can effectively control spending. About 70 percent of the budget is relatively fixed. Interest payments to those who hold government bonds must be paid. Significant reductions in Social Security benefits and appropriations for the Department of Defense are hard to achieve, given the political popularity of such expenditures and the fact that contracts have already been entered into by the government.

The budget itself only partially reflects the amount of government spending and borrowing that occur. Herman B. Leonard has identified six major forms of "quiet spending" that do not have to go through the appropriations process. These include promises to pay future retirement benefits for public employees, Social Security system benefits, federal loans and loan guarantees, tax subsidies (also known as "tax expenditures"), asset spend-down (the depreciated value of roads, buildings, and other aspects of the public infrastructure as a result of age and lack of maintenance), and long-term public leases of the facilities needed by government. Such forms of "back-door" borrowing or "off-line" spending have become commonplace in Washington.[17]

PERSPECTIVES ON FEDERAL SPENDING

There are several explanations of the functions and size of the federal budget. Economists and students of political economy differ about the reasons for, and the desirability of, the huge sums spent by the national government.

The Keynesians (those influenced by the ideas of the English economist John Maynard Keynes) believe that large government expenditures can help to stimulate the economy. When conditions are sluggish—unemployment is high and production is falling—they prescribe increased spending and lower taxes, even if that creates large deficits. Typically, they wish to reverse the process and ensure budget surpluses as a means of holding down inflation if the economy becomes overheated and demand seems excessive.[18]

Supply-siders, on the other hand, tend to favor low taxes and limited public expenditures. Economists and writers, such as Arthur Laffer and Jude Wanniski, believe that the best way to promote prosperity and hold down prices is to stimulate production and thereby increase the supply of goods and services. Public diversion of resources through high taxes, they argue, serves as a disincentive for businessowners and workers to put forth greater effort and invest more. Expenditures for social welfare are also generally viewed with suspicion, because supply-siders believe that they provide people with reasons not to work.[19]

Edward Tufte believes that the timing of expenditures is partly a function of the timing of elections. Tufte maintains that in the years of national elections the federal government will generally spend more to stimulate the economy, thereby encouraging higher levels of employment and greater income. This pattern of preelection spending is, of course, designed to help an incumbent president or his party win reelection. The electoral-economic cycle thus becomes a useful predictor of the fluctuations in government spending.[20]

DEFICIT REDUCTIONS

In recent years the size of the federal deficit has become a topic of great concern. In 1986, it reached $220.7 billion, or 5.3 percent of the gross national product (GNP).

The growing national debt and the ever-increasing deficits were perceived as serious problems for at least three reasons. First, the low individual savings rate of Americans, which fell below 4 percent in the mid to late 1980s, meant that large-scale borrowing by the federal government might crowd out money needed by business for necessary improvements in plant and equipment. If the United States had not attracted billions of dollars in foreign investments, part of which went to purchase federal securities, it is likely that the economy would have declined or stagnated during the past decade.

Second, the need for money to be funneled into the national treasury could serve to increase the rate of inflation. When combined with the low rate of domestic savings and the growing trade deficit (the excess value of imports over the value of exports), large federal deficits signal to investors here and abroad that Americans are living beyond their means. Because demand appears to be so great that the nation is willing to borrow heavily to meet its wants, there is a danger that interest rates will climb and the cost of consumer goods will begin to rise more rapidly. If foreign investors believe that inflation is likely to grow in the years ahead, they will either demand a higher rate of return for their money or, conceivably, they will stop sending their funds to the United States.

Third, interest on the national debt has come to represent a growing portion of the budget. Today, about one out of every seven dollars spent by the federal government is allotted for this purpose. These transfer payments go mainly to middle- and upper-income individuals and large financial institutions. Therefore, a significant part of the budget is spent not to help the poor or to provide services for all citizens. Rather, it is redistributed mostly to more prosperous purchasers of government securities, many of whom are not even residents of this country.[21]

The very existence of large budget deficits has made it more difficult to fund new programs or to maintain support for those which primarily assist low-income people, who have limited political influence. It has also caused Congress to try to reduce the gap between outlays and revenues.

The Gramm-Rudman-Hollings Act

In 1985, after months of unsuccessful and frustrating efforts to reduce ever-increasing budget deficits, Congress enacted a law designed to eliminate all deficits by fiscal 1991. The measure was introduced in September by two freshmen members of the Senate—Phil Gramm (Republican, Texas) and Warren B. Rudman (Republican, New Hampshire)—and a more senior member of that body, Ernest F. Hollings (Democrat, South Carolina).[22] The Balanced Budget and Emergency Deficit Control Act is now commonly called the Gramm-Rudman-Hollings Act.

Seven years before, Congress had actually written a requirement into law that, beginning in fiscal 1981, annual budget outlays were not to exceed the receipts of the federal government. This provision (which had been introduced by Senator Harry F. Byrd, Jr., Independent, Virginia) was mandatory, but members of a House–Senate conference committee, who were considering a bill to which this requirement was added, softened its effect by stating that it "could be suspended by the action of future Congresses." In 1980, Public Law 96-389 reaffirmed the congressional intent to balance the budget by fiscal 1981, but eliminated any mandatory requirement. Thus, the House and Senate weakened, and later ignored, their own previously enacted legislation.[23]

The impetus for Gramm-Rudman-Hollings came as a result of a joint resolution (House Joint Resolution 372) begun in the House of Representatives to raise the debt limit to $2.079 trillion. When it reached the Senate, two Republican members, Steven D. Symms of Idaho and William L. Armstrong of Colorado, expressed an interest in reviving fights over the budget as soon as the resolution was brought to the floor. On September 25, Senators Gramm, Rudman, and Hollings introduced their bill (Senate 1702), which set deficit targets for the next five fiscal years, required a balanced budget by fiscal 1991, and established a system of automatic spending cuts to meet the targets.[24]

On October 3, Senate Majority Leader Robert Dole, (Republican, Kansas) offered a version of Gramm-Rudman-Hollings as an amendment to House Joint Resolution 372. Within one week, the Senate passed the debt-limit resolution as amended by a vote of 51 to 37. However, the vote came only after one important change was adopted and several proposed alterations to the deficit reducing provisions were discussed.[25]

Democratic critics pointed out that major expenditures, such as federal farm price supports and multiyear procurement contracts for major weapons, were largely exempt from automatic cuts. Senators James Exon of Nebraska, John Kerry of Massachusetts, and Thomas Eagleton of Missouri sponsored unsuccessful amendments to make cuts more likely in November 1985, rather than having to wait for more than a year. An amendment was offered by David L. Boren (Democrat, Oklahoma), one of the sponsors of Gramm-Rudman-Hollings, to subject Social Security cost-of-living adjustments in part to automatic cuts, but it was tabled by a vote of 71 to 27.[26]

A key amendment by Carl Levin (Democrat, Michigan) was adopted by voice vote on October 9. Originally, the deficit-reduction plan required uniform cuts from OMB spending accounts, which often included many programs. The Levin amendment required that cuts come from individual programs, projects, or activities as defined by the most recently enacted appropriations measures, thus significantly limiting presidential discretion to shift the burden of automatic cuts within accounts.[27]

House Democratic leaders feared that with so much congressional pressure to pass a strong antideficit measure, there might be a rush to accept the Senate plan. Instead, on October 11 the House asked for a conference committee in hopes of altering the Senate measure. A group of 9 senators and 48 representatives were appointed to the conference, which sought answers from sponsors and staff about questions arising from the measure. Conferees wanted to know more about how the plan would work, whether it could be circumvented, whether it vested too much power in unelected bureaucrats at the expense of Congress, and whether it was constitutional.

After some discussion, House and Senate members of the conference committee continued to differ in their deficit limits, their reliance on the CBO and the OMB to calculate deficit projections, and in the way they treated Medicare and defense spending. Thus, the conference was deadlocked.[28]

After conference committee members failed to agree, a vote was taken in the House on House Joint Resolution 372 on November 1. The overwhelming majority of Democrats in that body, joined by Republican John Paul Hammerschmidt of Arkansas, voted 249 to 180 to substitute a very different version of the antideficit provisions. The Senate on November 6 voted again for its version, with some modifications, thus bringing about the creation of a second conference.

The second conference consisted of 66 members, 29 of whom constituted a working group. A smaller number of leaders, including Senate Budget Committee Chairman Pete V. Domenici (Republican, New Mexico), Senate Finance Committee Chairman Robert Packwood (Republican, Oregon), House Majority Whip Thomas S. Foley (Democrat, Washington), House Democratic Caucus Chairman Richard Gephardt of Missouri, Representative Les Aspin (Democrat, Wisconsin), and Representative Leon Panetta (Democrat, California), actually arrived at many of the compromises. Moreover, the measure's sponsors, particularly Senator Gramm, participated in negotiations.

By 1:00 A.M. on December 10, after extensive private talks, negotiators reached final agreement on the package of changes. Among the final points to be decided was a provision to give the president a limited degree of discretion to make defense cuts under the automatic procedure.[29]

Once the conference committee agreed to the final version of the plan, both houses approved the legislation on the evening of December 11. The Senate adopted the conference report by a 61 to 31 vote, rejecting a motion by Senator Jeremiah Denton (Republican, Alabama) that would have permitted the president to shield defense spending from the automatic spending cuts. The House voted 271 to 154 for the conference agreement. On December 12, the president signed House Joint Resolution 372 into law.[30]

The Gramm-Rudman-Hollings plan significantly altered budgetary procedures to reduce and eventually eliminate budget deficits. The following are its major provisions:

1. Required that budget deficits not exceed $171.9 billion in fiscal 1986, $144 billion in fiscal 1987, $108 billion in fiscal 1988, $72 billion in fiscal 1989, and $36 billion in fiscal 1990. A balanced budget was to be achieved in fiscal 1991.
2. Required across-the-board automatic cuts, known as sequestrations, from most programs by a uniform percentage to achieve deficit goals if these were not reached by regular budget and appropriations actions. Automatic cuts were to be divided equally between defense and nondefense expenditures.
3. Provided special rules for fiscal 1986 automatic cuts, which would go into effect March 1 and would be limited to $11.7 billion.
4. Exempted the following from automatic cuts: Social Security; interest on the federal debt; veterans' compensation and pensions; Medicaid; Aid to Families with Dependent Children (AFDC); the Women's, Infants', and Children's (WIC) food program; Supplemental Security Income (SSI); food stamps; and child nutrition. Cuts in five health programs, including Medicare, were to be limited.

5. Mandated that if the courts invalidated the mechanism triggering automatic cuts, which required action by the CBO, the OMB, and the General Accounting Office (GAO), the order for making these cuts would need approval by both houses of Congress and the president.
6. Authorized suspension of automatic cuts during a recession or war.
7. Established accelerated budget timetables and new procedures to prevent action on the floor to pass legislation which would be over the budget.[31]

There are important lessons to be learned from Gramm-Rudman-Hollings about the legislative process and the problems of controlling budget deficits. First, the legislation was passed in an atmosphere of high budgetary shortfalls, making it easier for members of Congress to vote for stringent, if gradual, reductions in spending. No one may have been completely satisfied with the provisions of the law, but it was seen as necessary. M. Wendell Belew, Jr., counsel to the House Budget Committee, said of the enforced cuts, "What they're doing is they're creating a kind of artificial crisis. It's an attempt to create an action-forcing mechanism."[32] One of the law's sponsors, Warren Rudman, remarked that it was "a bad idea whose time has come."[33]

Second, the passage of the budget-reduction plan shows the opportunities for both legislative entrepreneurship and important change by a small number of legislators. Three senators sponsored and initially pushed this measure. As we previously noted, Carl Levin, a member of the Democratic minority in the Senate, was responsible for an important amendment to the original proposal. Ultimately, differences in the House and Senate versions of the legislation were reconciled mainly by a small group of leaders in each house of Congress.

Third, the role of the president and administration representatives appears to have been decidedly less important than that of congressional leaders and activists in shaping this legislation. Although some members of the president's cabinet, including Treasury Secretary James A. Baker III, Defense Secretary Casper W. Weinberger, and Secretary of State George P. Schultz, were opposed to Gramm-Rudman-Hollings, the president endorsed the measure. The OMB negotiated with Congress and with Senator Phil Gramm, the leading proponent of the proposal, but Director James C. Miller III generally delegated the handling of daily discussions to assistants Timothy J. Muris and M. B. Oglesby. Because President Reagan endorsed the plan early in October, before provisions were finalized, he had a limited ability to alter the course of the legislation. In essence, he was endorsing a concept without knowing the details. For the most part, the administration was able to modify the proposal only slightly in order to reduce defense cuts under the automatic provisions of the bill and to postpone defense cuts in early 1986 while arms negotiators were meeting in Geneva.[34]

The reasons for the limited executive role on a bill of this importance are complex. Clearly, the legislation was a congressional initiative and reflected the desire of many members, particularly Republicans, to do something to curb future deficits. The administration itself was divided. The chief of staff, Donald T. Regan, and his top aide, W. Dennis Thomas, supported the measure and helped persuade the president to endorse it, despite the opposition of several cabinet members. The president's endorsement, however, came only after there were enough votes in the Senate to approve the original proposal. An early sign of support might have given the White House greater leverage to modify the measure according to its preferences; Reagan's statement came only a few days before Senate approval of the debt-raising resolution and its subsequent referral to a conference committee. Thus, he could not know or easily influence the final provisions of Gramm-Rudman-Hollings. During the period when the legislation was being considered, James C. Miller, a new director of OMB, was taking over, and he failed to become personally involved in many of the negotiations surrounding the details of the deficit-reduction plan. The president was preoccupied with foreign policy, most notably his meeting with Soviet leader Mikhail S. Gorbachev, while the second conference committee met to resolve differences between the House and the Senate.[35]

Finally, we should note that the legislation itself has had only a limited effect on reducing federal deficits. In 1986 the Supreme Court upheld the decision of a special three-judge panel of the federal district court in Washington, which stated that the role of the GAO, an arm of Congress, in ratifying the amount and scope of automatic, across-the-board cuts was unconstitutional because it violated the doctrine of separation of powers. Thus, the first round of cuts for fiscal 1986 were invalid, and the House and Senate had to adopt joint resolutions restoring the cuts.[36] So far, the budgeting guidelines set forth in Gramm-Rudman-Hollings have not been met (Table 3–2). The most that one can say is that there has been a gradual reduction in budgetary deficits since fiscal 1986. Perhaps the decision to pass deficit-reducing legislation has had the effect of lessening the gap between revenues and outlays, but that is speculation.

Other Methods of Reducing Deficits

Even without Gramm-Rudman-Hollings, mechanisms exist to secure deficit reductions. For example, the president can propose a balanced budget or one in which deficits are less than the year before. He can try to stay within those budgetary limits by threatening to veto legislation that greatly exceeds his recommendations. Under the Congressional Budget and Impoundment Control Act of 1974, the president can defer expenditures or even rescind them if the legislative branch goes along with his plans.[37]

In recent years members of the Reagan administration and some persons who simply wish to reduce large budgetary deficits have argued that entitlements must be curbed. Entitlements are programs that disburse money to various classes of people according to a right established by law. Although entitlements are an important part of the budget, some, such as the Social Security benefits paid to older people, disabled workers, and the children of deceased employees, are politically popular. So also are the cost-of-living adjustments for Social Security recipients. Therefore, it is more likely that Social Security taxes will be raised than that benefits will be reduced for many people. Somewhat greater success has been achieved in reducing monies for food stamps and other programs designed to help low-income people, but that means that a disproportionate share of the burden of deficit reduction tends to fall on those who probably are in greatest need of assistance.[38]

Two proposals to cut deficits gained prominence during the years of the Reagan presidency: a line-item veto and a constitutional amendment requiring a balanced budget. Ronald Reagan asked Congress to give him the authority to veto individual spending programs. At the present time the president must sign or veto an entire bill, and appropriations measures often combine a number of disparate programs. This proposal would give the president the same power possessed by most state governors. Critics have suggested that a line-item veto would alter the bargaining power of the two branches of government, to the detriment of Congress. Others have said that a constitutional amendment is required before such a change could occur.[39]

Proponents of a constitutional amendment to require a balanced budget argue that this is the only way to guarantee the elimination of deficits. Opponents maintain that it is unnecessary, ineffective, or dangerous. They say that a balanced budget could be achieved without an amendment to the Constitution. If, as is generally proposed, an extraordinary majority of members could suspend the requirement for a balanced budget in cases of recession, war, or other national emergency, then it would probably be ineffective. If there was an absolute requirement for a balanced budget, it could cause harm by forcing an increase in taxes or a cut in expenditures at a time when adverse economic conditions or crisis made deficit spending more rational.[40]

THE IMPORTANCE OF BALANCED BUDGETS

Most observers agree that large budget deficits at this time are undesirable. However, it is far less clear whether it is necessary to have balanced budgets each year.

Those who believe that fiscal policy should be used to stabilize the economy—stimulate employment and production or reduce inflation as conditions require—argue that deficits are appropriate in some years and surpluses in others. Another argument for "unbalanced" budgets is that we make no distinction between operating expenses and capital spending or investments. Perhaps the daily operations of government agencies should be financed on a pay-as-you-go basis, but isn't it appropriate to borrow money for construction of public works or investments in infrastructure (dams, highways, water treatment plants, and the like)? Certainly, state and local governments, as well as private corporations, often borrow for long-term projects.[41]

It is clear that federal budgets do not contain all public spending by the national government. As we noted earlier, there are several ways in which expenditures can go off budget or avoid the regular process of appropriations. Even within the budget there is some distortion. In the years of the Johnson administration, a unified budget was created, which combined Social Security expenditures with other government spending. Today, the surpluses in the Social Security trust fund serve to reduce the budget deficits even though monies cannot be spent for general public purposes.[42]

Even today's large deficits are not seen as equally dangerous by all economists. For example, Robert E. Hall argues that deficits are growing more slowly than the economy, and their very existence creates a climate in which free spending has declined. C. Fred Bergsten, on the other hand, believes that current budget deficits are dangerous, because we are simultaneously running large trade deficits and there is no reason to believe that we can continue to attract large amounts of foreign investment. Bergsten fears that the value of the dollar could be forced down excessively, thus causing a substantial rise in prices and interest rates.[43]

SUMMARY

This chapter has examined spending policy as a means of influencing the economy. We have looked at the budget as a political document that governs decisions concerning the allocation of national resources. The problem of budget deficits and some of the ways of dealing with them have also been considered.

There are a number of limits on the use of the budget as an instrument of fiscal control. There is no central authority responsible for all budgetary decisions. As we have noted, there are many actors within and outside the government who influence spending. Neither the president nor Congress can easily control the growth of such expenditures as interest on the debt or popular entitlements. In a sense, the iron triangle, which was mentioned in Chapter One, sets some limits on the extent of fiscal cuts. More powerful and aggressive interest groups and bureaucrats can be expected to work with relevant congressional committees to curb sharp reductions, even during periods when decrementalism is more characteristic of budgetary decision-aiming than incremental growth.

Even the passage of legislation, such as Gramm-Rudman-Hollings, to cut federal spending is no guarantee that balanced budgets will soon be the rule. Certainly, neither that bill nor other alternatives commonly discussed will eliminate many expenditures and additional obligations that are not part of the annual appropriations process.

Chapter Four, which considers tax policy, will discuss how we pay for the needs and wants that we recognize when the budget is proposed. Two important changes in tax law will be studied: the Economic Recovery Tax Act of 1981 and the Tax Reform Act of 1986.

NOTES

[1]Dwight D. Eisenhower, "The President's News Conference of February 9, 1955," *Public Papers of the Presidents, 1955* (Washington, DC: U.S. Government Printing Office, 1959), p. 256.

[2]John F. Kennedy, "Address to the American Society of Newspaper Editors," April 19, 1963, *Public Papers of the Presidents, 1963* (Washington, DC: U.S. Government Printing Office, 1964), p. 326.

[3]Louis W. Koenig, *The Chief Executive* (5th ed.; San Diego: Harcourt Brace Jovanovich, 1986), p. 182.

[4]*Ibid.*, p. 162.

[5]Richard E. Neustadt, "Presidency and Legislation: The Growth of Central Clearance," *American Political Science Review*, 48 (September 1954), pp. 641–671.

[6]Koenig, p. 182.

[7]Harvey S. Rosen, *Public Finance* (2d ed.; Homewood, IL.: Irwin, 1988), p. 117; and Howard E. Shuman, *Politics and the Budget: The Struggle Between the President and the Congress* (2d ed.; Englewood Cliffs, NJ: Prentice Hall, 1988), pp. 217–244.

[8]Shuman, p. 221.

[9]For a discussion of PPB, see Aaron Wildavsky, *The Politics of The Bugetary Process* (4th ed.; Boston: Little, Brown, 1984), pp. 186–202.

[10]*Ibid.*, pp. 202–207.

[11]Expertise and specialization are important values that tend to be cultivated and respected by members of Congress. The need for experienced and knowledgeable sifting of legislation has helped to give congressional committees their power. William J. Keefe and Morris S. Ogul, *The American Legislative Process: Congress and the States* (3d ed.; Englewood Cliffs, NJ: Prentice Hall, 1973), pp. 155–157.

[12]Randall B. Ripley, *Congress: Process and Policy* (2d ed., New York: W. W. Norton & Co., Inc., 1978), pp. 124–125.

[13]For a discussion of incrementalism, see Charles E. Lindblom, "The Science of 'Muddling Through,'" *Public Administration Review*, 19 (Spring 1959), pp. 79–88; and Otto A. Davis, M. A. H. Dempster, and Aaron Wildavsky, "A Theory of the Budgetary Process," *American Political Science Review*, 60 (September 1966), pp. 529–547.

[14]Allen Schick, "Incremental Budgeting in a Decremental Age," *Policy Sciences*, 16 (September 1983), pp. 1–25.

[15]"$576 Billion Omnibus Funding Bill Approved, "*Congressional Quarterly Almanac*, 1986 (Washington, DC: Congressional Quarterly, 1987), pp. 219–221.

[16]Despite some important cuts during Reagan's first year in office, Paul E. Peterson and Mark Rom maintain that Reagan was able only to check the growth of safety-net programs, not really to cut them back. "Lower Taxes, More Spending, and Budget Deficits," in Charles O. Jones, ed., *The Reagan Legacy: Promise and Performance* (Chatham, NJ: Chatham House, 1988), pp. 226–227.

[17]Such agencies as the Tennessee Valley Authority are permitted to issue bonds of their own, but they usually borrow money through the Federal Financing Bank

(FFB), a body created in 1974. It can issue bonds up to a statutory limit authorized by Congress, or it can borrow directly from the Treasury. Herman B. Leonard, *Checks Unbalanced: The Quiet Side of Public Spending* (New York: Basic Books, 1986), pp. 7–11, 96.

[18]For a discussion of Keynes's work, *The General Theory of Employment, Interest, and Money*, see Robert L. Heilbroner, *The Worldly Philosophers: The Lives, Times, and Ideas of the Great Economic Thinkers* (6th ed.; New York: Simon & Schuster, 1986), pp. 274–281.

[19]See *Supply-Side Economics in the 1980s: Conference Proceedings, Federal Reserve Bank of Atlanta* (Westport, CT: Quorum, 1982); and Victor A. Canto, Douglas H. Joines, and Arthur B. Laffer, *Foundations of Supply-Side Economics: Theory and Evidence* (New York: Academic Press, 1983).

[20]Edward R. Tufte, *Political Control of the Economy* (Princeton, NJ: Princeton University Press, 1978), pp. 3–64. Tufte maintains that in most of the democracies that he studied, there was an acceleration of real income growth in election years.

[21]In fact, most federal government securities are still owned by Americans. Only about 14 percent of the federal debt held by the public was owned by foreigners in 1987. Executive Office of the President, Office of Management and Budget, *Special Analyses: Budget of the United States Government, Fiscal Year 1989* (Washington, DC: U.S. Government Printing Office, 1988), p. E-15.

[22]"Congress Enacts Strict Anti-Deficit Measure," *Congressional Quarterly Alamanac 1985* (Washington, DC: Congressional Quarterly, 1986), p. 459.

[23]*Ibid.*, p. 460

[24]*Ibid.*, pp. 466–467.

[25]*Ibid.*, p. 467.

[26]*Ibid.*

[27]*Ibid.*

[28]*Ibid.*, pp. 467–468.

[29]*Ibid.*, p. 468.

[30]*Ibid.*

[31]*Ibid.*, p. 459

[32]Jonathan Rauch and Richard E. Cohen, "Budget Frustration Boiling Over," *National Journal*, 17 (October 12, 1985), p. 2318.

[33]"Congress Enacts Strict Anti-Deficit Measure," p. 459.

[34]Dick Kirschten and Jonathan Rauch, "Political Poker Game Over Deficit Bill Calls Bluff of Reagan and Congress," *National Journal*, 17 (December 14, 1985), pp. 2855–2860.

[35]*Ibid.* and "Congress Enacts Strict Anti-Deficit Measure," p. 468.

[36]"Gramm-Rudman: A Year of Mixed Success," *Congressional Quarterly Almanac 1986* (Washington, DC: Congressional Quarterly, 1987), p. 579.

[37]For a discussion of the procedures of a *deferral* of funds (when they are temporarily withheld or delayed) or a *recission* (when funds in whole or in part cannot be used at all), see Shuman, pp. 240–243.

[38]The extent of the impact of Reagan administration policies is a matter of dispute. See, for example, Peterson and Rom, pp. 213–240; and Executive Office of the President, Office of Management and Budget, *The United States Budget in Brief, Fiscal Year 1989* (Washington, DC: U.S. Government Printing Office, 1988), p. 4.

[39]"Line-Item Veto Fails," *Congressional Quarterly Almanac 1985* (Washington, DC: Congressional Quarterly, 1986), pp. 468–469.

[40]For a discussion of the arguments for and against a balanced-budget amendment, see the October 1982 issue of *Congressional Digest*, particularly pp. 227–255.

[41]For a consideration of capital budgeting, see *Strengthening the Federal Budget Process: A Requirement for Effective Fiscal Control* (Washington, DC: Committee for Economic Development, 1983), pp. 42–53.

[42]Those who defend the inclusion of Social Security and other trust funds in determining deficits point out that trust fund surpluses can be invested only in Treasury securities. David Rapp, "The Social Security Surplus: A Snare...Or an Incentive for Deficit Reduction," *Congressional Quarterly Weekly Report* (November 26, 1988), pp. 3382–3383.

[43]Robert E. Hall and C. Fred Bergsten, "Are Deficits Sinking the Economy?" *New York Times*, December 21, 1988, p. A35.

CHAPTER FOUR

Taxing Policy

Two essential facts are critical to understanding the historical development of the income tax in the United States. The first is the importance of periods of war; and the second is the incremental process of change which shapes tax policy.[1]

John F. Witte

FEDERAL TAX COLLECTIONS: AN OVERVIEW

The history of federal taxation in the United States confirms two commonly held beliefs: that tax receipts have increased greatly since the national government first began to operate, and that the increases have been most dramatic during the twentieth century (See Table 4–1). It also shows that the sources of budgetary receipts have changed significantly during the last two centuries. How does one explain these changes? The growth of federal taxes is undoubtedly related to a 60-fold increase in population, rising costs in providing public services, and an even greater increment in the nation's wealth. However, it is also closely associated with the performance of new government functions and the creation of a system of revenue collection based on the income of individuals and corporations.

In 1789 the new government of the United States did not have to concern itself with Social Security payments or with a wide array of health and welfare benefits. It could rely on customs duties to provide almost all of the funds needed to pay interest on the public debt and to carry out the other obligations with which it was charged.

A growing concern with fairness in the distribution of the tax burden and the need for additional revenue to perform the functions of the modern state led to calls for the passage of an income tax. For a short time during the Civil War, Congress had adopted an income tax as an emergency measure. After the war, the tax was repealed. Later in the nineteenth century, Congress passed a tax on individual incomes, only to have the Supreme Court declare the statute unconstitutional because it was a direct

TABLE 4–1 Federal Budget Receipts, Selected Years 1789–1990 (in millions of dollars)

Year	Budget Receipts
1789–1791	4.4
1800	10.8
1810	9.4
1820	17.9
1830	24.8
1840	19.5
1850	43.6
1860	56.1
1870	411.3
1880	333.5
1890	403.1
1900	567.2
1910	675.5
1920	6,648.9
1930	4,057.9
1940	6,400
1950	39,500
1960	92,492
1970	192,800
1980	517,100
1990	1,073,451 (estimated)

Sources: *Historical Statistics, Colonial Times to 1970*, Part 2, (Washington, DC: U.S. Government Printing Office, 1975), Series Y 335–338, pp. 1104–1105. *Statistical Abstract of the United States, 1982–83* (Washington, DC: U.S. Government Printing Office, 1982), p. 246; and *Budget of the United States Government, Fiscal Year 1991*, (Washington, DC: U.S. Government Printing Office, 1990), p. A-281.

tax, which had to be levied in direct proportion to the population of the states. As a result of the *Pollock* decision,[2] the Constitution had to be amended if an income tax was to be imposed. The Sixteenth Amendment, ratified in 1913, permitted Congress "to lay and collect taxes on incomes, from whatever source derived ...."[3]

Although the individual income tax was originally collected from only a small proportion of the working population, it rapidly grew in importance as a source of revenue. By 1925 the taxes on individual and corporate income provided over half of the receipts for the national government.[4]

Changes in the rates of taxation have varied, but taxes generally increase in time of war. Of course, budget deficits often grow even more rapidly.

ACTORS INVOLVED IN MAKING TAX POLICY

Although the Constitution authorizes Congress "to lay and collect taxes," the making of tax policy is in fact a collaborative effort. Congress, the president and his chief advisers in the executive branch, certain bureaucrats, and representatives of many interest groups are prominent actors in the process.

The House of Representatives is usually more influential than the Senate in this policy area, because revenue bills must originate there. The Ways and Means Committee (Figure 4–1) is the body within the House that is responsible for considering proposed tax legislation. Its staff will almost always be involved in helping to draft changes in controversial bills. The committee draws most of its membership from the wealthier and more populous states.

The counterpart of the House Ways and Mean Committee is the Senate Finance Committee. It is a smaller body than Ways and Means, and its members, representing states rather than congressional districts, are likely to be concerned with a somewhat broader range of interests. The staff also contributes its expertise in writing and modifying tax measures. The Ways and Means Committee and the Finance Committee are aided by staff members from the Joint Committee on Taxation.[5]

Before a tax bill can become law, it must be passed by both houses of Congress. Should the House and Senate disagree on the final version of a measure, a conference committee is formed consisting of members of both houses, who try to reconcile the differences. Members of the conference committee from the House are appointed by the Speaker, and those from the Senate are named by the majority leader. The conference committee includes the chairpersons and some of the more influential members of the Ways and Means and Finance committees. Both political parties are represented.

Figure 4–1 House Ways and Means Committee.

Given the fact that the president can veto a tax bill, he becomes an important part of the bargaining process concerned with its passage. Moreover, as the head of the executive branch, nominal leader of one of the major parties, and the only person aside from the vice-president to be elected nationally, he is looked to for leadership on important legislation. Indeed, he helps to set the policy agenda.

Before making specific recommendations on tax legislation, the president would probably consult with at least three officials—the secretary of the Treasury, the director of the Office of Management and Budget (OMB), and the chairperson of the Council of Economic Advisers (CEA). Only the chairperson of the CEA is likely to be a professional economist. These officials would indicate which alternatives they thought were politically and economically feasible.

In addition to key presidential advisers there are many members of the bureaucracy, some of whom are career civil servants, who influence the writing of the tax code. We have already noted that the staffs of the House Ways and Means and Senate Finance committees will provide technical information and assist in the drafting of legislation in accordance with the wishes of the members of those bodies. The commissioner of Internal Revenue, who heads the Internal Revenue Service (IRS), and the assistant secretary of the Treasury for Tax Policy are among those likely to be involved in the making of tax law. Moreover, the IRS plays a major role in enforcing acts of Congress, particularly through its power to make rules and interpret the tax code.[6]

Taxes affect everyone in the nation because they determine the share of national expenditures that all must bear, and they provide incentives or disincentives for economic activity. Thus, it is not surprising that lobbyists for a myriad of business, agricultural, trade, professional, and labor organizations descend on Congress whenever major revisions of the tax code are contemplated. The National Association of Manufacturers, the U.S. Chamber of Commerce, the Farm Bureau, and the AFL-CIO are among the more prominent interest groups that participate in formulating policy.

ISSUES INVOLVED IN TAX POLICY

There are numerous issues involved in establishing tax policy for a country as large and diverse as the United States. Every time a new tax is imposed or tax rates are changed, there are winners and losers. The issues we will consider in this section are among the broader ones of concern to most citizens and policy-makers alike.

1. How high should taxes be, and who should bear the burden? At some point taxes can become so high that either citizens refuse to do additional work and invest, or they seek ways of avoiding these payments. Unfortunately, it isn't clear exactly when that point will be reached. Americans pay approximately one-third of what they earn in taxes to federal, state, and local governments. Many Europeans pay 40 percent or more of their earnings in taxes. Indeed, some countries (Sweden and Israel, for example) take more than half of their citizens' income.

The general tendency in the United States in recent years has been to reduce the marginal tax rates—the percentage of earnings paid in taxes on the final increment of income. The 1986 Tax Reform Act reduced the maximum tax rates, so that the highest percentage that anyone will pay will gradually fall to 28 percent. Six years before, the highest rate of income taxation was 70 percent. Of course, the existence of many tax shelters—legal provisions permitting people to escape the full effects of taxation—allowed most persons in the highest brackets to pay much less than that very high percentage. Thus, the effective rates of taxation were less than the nominal or official rates.[7]

Just as important as the rates of taxation is the question of how the tax burden should be shared. A tax can be proportional, regressive, or progressive. A **proportional** tax is one that takes the same percentage of income from all taxpayers, regardless of earnings. A flat-rate income tax is a proportional levy, although some of the proposals for "flat-rate" taxes were actually only efforts to reduce the number of tax brackets. **Regressive** taxes take a higher percentage of income from the poor or persons of modest means than from the more affluent. Excise and sales taxes are almost always regressive; despite the publicity given to a small number of wealthy persons who pay no income taxes, the taxation of personal income is rarely regressive. A **progressive** tax is one with graduated rates; it takes a higher percentage of income as earnings increase. The federal income tax is progressive, although the degree of progressvity has been reduced as the number of tax brackets has declined.

Those who favor progressive taxes argue that wealthier people should pay a higher proportion of their income to the government because they can better afford to do so than less affluent individuals, who must spend most of their income for necessities. Thus the total tax burden will be borne more fairly.

Opponents of progressive taxation believe that it is unjust to impose disproportionate burdens on people as a result of their financial success; some see it as negating the principle of equality. Other objections include the fact that it complicates the structure of the income tax, encouraging people to find ways to avoid taxes and obfuscating questions of equity among taxpayers; that it is politically irresponsible because the majority can impose very high rates of taxation on a minority of citizens; and that it may lessen the economic productivity of society by discouraging extra effort.[8]

Few people intellectually defend the concept of regressivity. However, some advocates of excise taxes, particularly taxes on alcohol and tobacco, argue that they are justified because these products are "luxuries" and are also socially harmful. Therefore, it is suggested that such taxes could regulate their use, raise additional revenue, and yet not deny people the necessities of life. Excise taxes on gasoline at the pump are sometimes seen as user taxes, which not only provide money for the upkeep and construction of the nation's highways but also encourage fuel conservation. Proponents of a value-added tax, a kind of national sales tax that imposes a levy on the additional value of goods at various stages of production and exchange, argue that it would encourage savings and investment.[9]

2. Should taxes be used to promote economic growth? We have already seen that taxes are imposed for reasons other than simply raising revenue. Many economists believe that taxes can promote or deter economic growth and stability. Let us consider two schools of economic thought.

The Keynesians—followers of the twentieth-century British economist John Maynard Keynes—argue that government should stimulate the economy during periods of low production and high unemployment by lowering taxes and raising public expenditures. When the economy is overheated—production and employment are at their height and prices are rising rapidly—the process should be reversed. Then, government should raise taxes and lower expenditures. Government would be running a deficit during "bad" times (i.e., times of recession) and a surplus when times were too "good" (i.e., periods of high inflation). During the entire course of the economic cycle, it is hoped, the budget would be balanced. By a judicious use of taxing and spending policy, the Keynesians argue, excessive unemployment and runaway inflation could be avoided.[10]

Critics of Keynesian economics suggest that too often in the past, presidents and members of Congress have been more willing to lower taxes and raise expenditures to stimulate the economy than to reverse the process when inflationary pressures mounted. They blame Keynesian policies for the rising public debt. Of course, it could be argued that the inadequate execution of Keynesian ideas, rather than the underlying theory behind them, has caused this problem. There are, however, more basic criticisms. It isn't always clear when taxes and public expenditures should be raised or lowered during the economic cycle. In the mid-1970s and early 1980s, we seemed to be in a period of **stagflation**, when there was relatively low economic growth and high inflation. Clearly, Keynes did not anticipate this condition. Can government be trusted to use taxing and spending policies to stimulate or control economic growth? Does it have the knowledge to do so?[11]

Supply-side economists, such as Arthur Laffer, argue that a major weakness of Keynesian economics is that it concentrates on demand—people's desire for goods and services and their ability to purchase them. Supply-siders maintain that the focus of government policy should be on increasing the supply of goods and services, thus increasing employment and holding prices in check. They suggest that the supply can be expanded by increasing rewards and reducing disincentives for the productive members of society. By lowering taxes to a level that is generally acceptable, people are encouraged to work harder because they can keep most of what they earn. When tax rates are very high, either people will cease to do more or they will try to evade paying the government what is legally required. When taxes are lowered to an acceptable level, production and revenues will increase.[12] The 1981 tax act, which lowered income tax rates by approximately 25 percent, was justified on the basis of supply-side arguments.[13]

Those who disagree with supply-side economics believe that it can greatly increase deficits, at least in the short run. Lowering tax rates may also do more to help the most affluent members of society than to stimulate production. There is not a specific rate generally agreed upon when taxes are so high that economic activity is discouraged. There is little evidence to indicate that lowering taxes will greatly increase investment and economic growth. Critics point to record deficits and modest gains in overall production during the 1980s to support their contention that supply-side theories have not been proven correct.[14]

3. Should taxes be used to help particular segments of the economy? Over the years the tax system in the United States has changed in many ways. Not only were tax rates raised or lowered, but special concessions were granted and new levies were imposed as well. Often these changes reflected a desire to alter economic policy so that certain sectors would be aided. Thus, when protective tariffs were imposed, it was hoped that new manufacturing industries would prosper. Depreciation allowances for oil companies and mineral-extraction firms were designed to provide incentives for producers.

Two issues arise when we consider the use of tax policy to promote particular sectors of the economy. First, we should ask who should be benefited. Some argue that today those industries that have been most adversely affected by competition from abroad, such as steel, automobiles, and rubber products, should be the principal beneficiaries of tax concessions. Others believe that the communications and electronics industries, which will provide many jobs in the future, should be encouraged by tax breaks.[15] The question of providing help through the tax structure involves regional struggles. Heavy industry has been mostly concentrated in the "rustbelt" states of the Northeast and Midwest, whereas the newer electronics and computer industries have tended to settle in the West and South.

A second more basic issue involves whether economic choices should be deliberately made through the taxing mechanism. Those who believe that it is correct to do so suggest that our economic base must be protected if we are to maintain our standard of living. Sometimes they also argue that national security considerations require the preservation of certain basic industries, and tax incentives, as well as trade regulations, are appropriate means of accomplishing this end.

Opponents of this position point out that not only manufacturers faced with foreign competition but virtually all occupations and professions seek tax advantages. Everyone claims a special need or a unique circumstance. Those interests with well-funded political action committees have often been most successful in getting what they wanted. Concessions for some industries and professions have meant higher taxes for others. It is better to allow the market to allocate winners and losers in the economic sphere than to have government favor some players over others.[16]

4. Should the tax code be used to ameliorate social problems? Just as there is disagreement over the desirability of taxes being used to help particular segments of the economy, so there are conflicts over using them to reduce social problems. In fact, tax breaks are already given for many purposes considered socially desirable. Deductions or tax credits are provided for charitable contributions, health insurance, child care, employee stock option plans, and many other activities.

Supporters of this strategy maintain that tax incentives help to strengthen the private, nonprofit sector; permit greater voluntary decision-making; and allow for experimentation in dealing with difficult societal problems. Opponents argue that taxes should be used to raise revenues, not to push people toward particular modes of behavior. Tax benefits for desirable activities inevitably lead to disparities, with some people or businesses paying a higher proportion of what they earn to the government because they have not adopted behaviors that meet the standards found in the tax code. If government considers particular activities desirable, it should either mandate them or provide them at public expense. It would then be easier to target the beneficiaries of a program and to measure its success.[17]

TAX POLICY: INCREMENTAL OR BASIC CHANGE?

Many changes in the federal tax laws have been characterized as gradual, piecemeal, or incremental alternatives. The conventional wisdom has been that the tax code is modified very slowly in response to pressures from interest groups and the bureaucracy, as well as by recognition on the part of the president and Congress that more revenue is needed or that the economy must be stimulated by tax cuts. In recent years, however, two major changes in federal tax policy have been made that seem to suggest that the executive and legislative branches can fashion laws that basically alter tax policy: the 1981 tax reduction and the 1986 Tax Reform Act.

1981 Tax Reduction

When Ronald Reagan was running for president in 1980, he endorsed a proposal for a major cut in federal income taxes. A bill originally introduced by Senator William V. Roth (Republican, Delaware) and Representative Jack F. Kemp (Republican, New York) was designed to reduce individual income taxes by about 33 percent over a three-year period, provide for future indexing of taxes to offset inflation, and create cuts in business taxes. When Republicans in Congress gave their support to a revised version of the Kemp-Roth bill, which would provide a one-year tax cut of 10 percent for individuals and faster business write-offs for investments in plants and equipment, Reagan endorsed this measure. He urged a tax cut for January 1, 1981, followed by the additional 10-percent cuts in individual income taxes in each of the next two years as well as indexing. Later that year Reagan backed a bill approved by the Senate Finance Committee that would have cut income taxes by $39 billion and provided incentives for business investment.[18]

After he became president, Ronald Reagan continued his call for a major reduction in taxes. On February 18, 1981, the president called for $53.9 billion in tax cuts in 1982. His plan would begin with a 10-percent cut in individual income tax rates on July 1, 1981 and provided additional 10-percent cuts on July 1 in each of the following two years. He dropped the idea of indexing but retained a business depreciation plan. He said that a second bill would provide relief to married couples from the "penalty" that current law imposed. For several months the administration refused to compromise. As a result of budgetary constraints and a lack of congressional support, Reagan on June 4, 1981, offered an alternative. He proposed $37.4 billion in tax cuts for 1982, agreed that the first annual reduction would be 5 percent to begin on October 1, 1981, and included such popular proposals as savings incentives and "marriage penalty" relief.[19]

Business groups were still unenthusiastic about the measure. Before the bill encompassing the June 4 alternative was introduced by Representatives Barber B. Conable, Jr. (Republican, New York) and Kent Hance (Democrat, Texas), the administration added more tax advantages for business. On July 24, 1981, only a few days before a close vote in the House was scheduled, the administration proposed its final legislation. Although across-the-board cuts and investment incentives remained, a host of new "sweeteners" was added in order to secure a limited number of swing votes in the House.[20]

The administration measure did not proceed through Congress without many alterations. The Senate Finance Committee sought to pressure the House Ways and Means Committee to act quickly on tax legislation, and attached a tax-cut package to a House debt-limit measure, thus allowing the circumvention of the constitutional requirement that all revenue-raising measures originate in the House. Despite objections from minority Democratic members Bill Bradley of New Jersey and George Mitchell of Maine that the administration bill was designed to help the rich, rather than those in the middle-income brackets, the committee approved the basic features of Reagan's plan. It approved a three-year, 25-percent across-the-board cut in individual income tax rates and an accelerated depreciation plan for business.[21]

The committee also agreed with the president to lower the top tax rate individuals pay on investment income to 50 percent. It accepted administration proposals to reduce the marriage penalty, increase deductions for contributions to individual retirement plans, and allow a 25-percent tax credit for wages paid for research and development. It reduced estate and gift taxes and increased tax relief for American workers overseas, for rehabilitation of old buildings, and for small oil producers subject to the windfall profit tax.[22]

The House Ways and Means Committee began in mid-June to create a substantially different bill from that proposed by the administration. It agreed to cut corporate tax rates, established a somewhat different system for depreciating real estate, accepted administration proposals to increase contributions to retirement plans for individuals and the self-employed, cut small-business taxes, and substituted for the president's tax cut proposal a two-year, 15-percent reduction.[23]

In the Senate the Finance Committee measure was amended in 12 days of debate. The Senate agreed to index individual income taxes beginning in 1985 to offset the effects of inflation. It allowed savings and loans, credit unions, and commercial banks to issue one-year tax-exempt savings certificates. An amendment by Republican Bob Packwood of Oregon to allow those who did not itemize deductions on their tax returns to take a deduction for charitable contributions was overwhelmingly adopted.[24]

The House accepted an administration substitute for the Ways and Means bill after the president made a successful televised appeal for public support on July 27.

On July 29, some 48 Democrats defected to support the Reagan proposal. Only one Republican, James Jeffords of Vermont, voted in opposition, and the measure was approved by a vote of 238 to 195.[25]

The conference committee had to resolve only a few major disagreements. Differences were resolved over tax breaks for oil royalty owners, while the House accepted Senate-passed child-care credits and increased tax benefits for employee stock ownership plans. The Senate accepted House-passed tax breaks for homes that were sold.[26]

The Economic Recovery Tax Act of 1981 was approved by Congress on August 4 and signed into law by the president on August 13. The law contained many major provisions, among the most important of which were the following:[27]

1. Reduced all individual income tax rates by 5 percent effective as of October 1, 1981, 10 percent as of July 1, 1982, and another 10 percent as of July 1, 1983.
2. Reduced the top rate on investment income from 70 percent to 50 percent, the maximum for earned income.
3. Reduced the maximum rate on capital gains from 28 percent to 20 percent effective as of June 10, 1981.
4. Provided for indexing of tax brackets to take into account annual increases in the cost of living (the consumer price index).
5. Allowed additional deductions for two-earner married couples filing joint returns in 1982.

1986 Tax Reform Act

The Tax Reform Act of 1986 was influenced by many factors: executive recommendations, legislative attempts at tax reform, and activities by lobbyists and average citizens. Without the president's persistent efforts, however, it is doubtful that the law would have been enacted.

The genesis of the new law was complex. Earlier proposals for lowering tax rates, reducing the number of tax brackets, and eliminating loopholes had been set forth by a number of members of Congress. For example, Senator Bill Bradley (Democrat, New Jersey) and Representative Richard Gephardt (Democrat, Missouri) introduced a reform measure in 1982 that would have lowered the top tax rate to 30 percent. The Bradley-Gephardt bill was reintroduced in 1983 and 1985. A "Fair and Simple Tax Act of 1985" was introduced in January 1985 by Representative Jack Kemp (Republican, New York) and Senator Bob Kasten (Republican, Wisconsin). The Kemp-Kasten bill would have encouraged more fairness through rate reduction and the elimination of tax breaks.[28]

Despite the legislation that had been introduced in Congress and the critical comments concerning the tax code that had been made in years past, most of the previous changes in tax law had been incremental. It was not until the Reagan administration proposed sweeping changes and worked actively to arouse interest in tax reform that major alterations were made. The Economic Recovery Tax Act of 1981 had already dramatically lowered tax rates, particularly for those in the highest income brackets. In his State of the Union message in 1984, Reagan said, "I am asking Secretary Don Regan for a plan for action to simplify the entire tax code, so all taxpayers, big and small, are treated more fairly. And I believe such a plan could result in that underground economy being brought into the sunlight of honest tax compliance. And it would make the tax base broader, so personal tax rates could come down, not go up."[29]

At the end of November, after the presidential election, the administration released a proposal, *Tax Reform for Fairness, Simplicity and Growth*, which became known as Treasury I. Like the Bradley-Gephardt bill, it would broaden the tax base while eliminating most credits, deductions, and exclusions. It also suggested a lowering of tax rates.[30]

This first plan was highly controversial. It would greatly limit or eliminate some popular deductions, such as those for state and local taxes and for charitable contributions. For example, only charitable deductions that exceeded 2 percent of taxable income could be claimed. State and local taxes would no longer be deductible. Treasury I would also have eliminated the payment of personal income tax for many low-income individuals and families. The highest personal income tax rate would be 35 percent, and there would be only 3, instead of 16, brackets.

The original Treasury plan called for a uniform tax rate for corporations and the end of certain tax breaks for business. Accelerated tax depreciation, which permitted companies to write off investments in new plants and equipment in a relatively short period, would be done away with; so also would the investment tax credit, which allowed firms to recover part of the cost of new equipment immediately in the form of lower taxes. Although corporate tax rates would be lowered to a single rate of 33 percent rather than a maximum of 46 percent, corporations collectively would pay approximately $22 billion more in 1986, about the same amount that individual income taxes would be reduced. The effect of these changes would be to shift more of the burden to corporate taxpayers. It would also significantly raise taxes for heavy industries, such as steel, that invest substantial sums of money in capital equipment.[31]

Early in January 1985, White House Chief of Staff James A. Baker III and Secretary of the Treasury Donald T. Regan announced their intentions to switch positions. Thus, Baker would become the administration spokesman on tax reform.[32]

In his State of the Union Address on February 6, 1985, the president said that tax reform would be at the top of his list of domestic priorities. Later that month the House Ways and Means Committee, chaired by Representative Dan Rostenkowski (Democrat, Illinois), began hearings on tax reform. On May 9, 1985, Senator Bob Packwood (Republican, Oregon) began hearings on tax reform in his Senate Finance Committee.[33]

On May 28, 1985, the administration announced a revised tax plan, the *President's Tax Proposals to the Congress for Fairness, Growth, and Simplicity*. This second plan was more politically acceptable, but it retained many of the features of Treasury I, including the reduction of brackets, the maximum rate of 35 percent, and the end of the deductions for state and local taxes.[34]

In response to the administration's plan, the House Ways and Means Committee and the Senate Finance Committee resumed hearings. Most attention was focused on the Ways and Means Committee because Congressman Rostenkowski wanted consideration for his own proposal as markup (the process of deciding on specific provisions and language of a legislative measure) began.[35]

After 28 days and almost 450 witnesses, public hearings came to an end. Markup soon began in closed sessions of the Ways and Means Committee, which were often attended by officials from the Treasury Department. At first members refused to give up their favored tax breaks, and it was only after Rostenkowski began to bargain with individual members, trading concessions for support of the entire proposal, that concern for tax reform again showed strength.[36]

On November 23, 1985, the Ways and Means Committee approved a compromise proposal by a vote of 28 to 9. All of the opposing votes were cast by Republicans. The proposal was introduced on the House floor the following week.

The Republicans introduced an alternative measure cosponsored by some minority members of the Ways and Means Committee. This bill received little support.[37]

Final passage of the Democratic tax reform bill was almost thwarted after the president gave only mild support for the proposal. The House voted 223 to 202 on December 11, 1985, to reject a rule that would have allowed the legislation to come to the floor. Only 14 Republicans voted in favor of the rule.

In order to prevent the defeat of tax reform, the president appealed to House Republicans, promising to insist upon changes in the Senate. On December 17, 1985, the House voted 256 to 171 to allow debate to begin. The bill was approved on a voice vote eight hours later.[38]

The bill approved by the House differed in some important respects from the administration's proposal. It imposed a higher maximum tax rate—38 percent—on individuals and eliminated some incentives for business investment. It set a maximum corporate tax rate at 36 percent and permitted corporate income below $75,000 to be taxed at lower rates. State and local sales, property, and income tax deductions were retained.[39]

Many Washington insiders still believed that tax reform was unlikely to occur. The Senate Finance Committee was seen as a probusiness fortress headed by a politician who had in the past favored tax breaks for a variety of economic interests. Lobbyists with connections to prominent members of the House and Senate, including persons who had once worked for Congressman Rostenkowski, Senator Russell Long of Louisiana, Senate Majority Leader Robert Dole of Kansas, and Senator Lloyd Bentsen of Texas, had tried to influence members in both chambers in 1985 and 1986. They sought concessions for banks, steel companies, and many other industries. Fundraisers were held as political action committees distributed campaign contributions to legislators seeking reelection.[40]

Clearly, the Republican-controlled Senate would seek a somewhat different approach to tax reform. The Senate rejected the House bill as a result of strong

Republican opposition. Chairman Packwood offered his own proposal for markup. Members of the committee voted again and again to retain existing tax breaks. Faced with the likelihood of another revenue-losing vote, Senator Packwood withdrew his proposal and adjourned the Committee on April 18, 1986. This deadlock could have led to the end of tax reform.

Instead, Packwood and his staff immediately sought to revise the plan. On April 24, he returned with a new package, one which would drop rates drastically (the new tax rates would be 15 to 25 percent). Thus, he hoped that committee members would be willing to give up their favored tax provisions.

Days of negotiations in executive sessions followed. On May 7, 1986, shortly after midnight, the Finance Committee approved a final reform measure by a vote of 20 to 0. The committee package called for individual tax rates of 15 percent and 27 percent, with a top corporate rate of 33 percent. After three weeks of debate and almost 50 minor amendments adopted on the floor, the Senate passed the Finance Committee measure on June 24, 1986, by a vote of 97 to 3. The major provisions of the bill remained unscathed.[41]

A Conference Committee, consisting of 11 senators and 11 representatives, began deliberations to reconcile differences between the House and Senate bills on July 17, 1986. It became clear that the entire conference could not agree, and the House and Senate members split up into caucuses, exchanging proposals for several weeks. Finally, there was agreement to let the two chairmen, Rostenkowski and Packwood, negotiate directly. After long meetings and negotiations, they presented a compromise measure to the Conference Committee, which voted 17 to 5 in favor of passage on August 16, 1986.[42]

Additional debate took place in the House and Senate over such diverse matters as the effects of the tax bill on business, its impact on Individual Retirement Accounts (IRAs), and the absence of sales tax deductions. On September 25, 1986, the House approved the measure by a vote of 292 to 136. Two days later, the Senate voted 74 to 23 in favor of the bill. Neither side adopted any amendments on the floor.[43]

Normally, when complex tax legislation is enacted, there are technical errors that need to be corrected. These enrolling corrections are usually offered in the form of a House concurrent resolution to handle mistakes made in the drafting process. The House passed the measure, but several members of the Senate tried to use the legislation to change substantive provisions of the tax law. Both houses adjourned before a compromise could be agreed upon, thus leaving some of the errors to be addressed in the next Congress.[44]

The president signed the tax bill into law on October 22, 1986. The Tax Reform Act of 1986 is an enormously complex measure. The following are some of its major provisions:[45]

1. **Lowering of individual income tax rates.** There would be two rates, 15 percent and 28 percent. The lower rate would be phased out for high-income taxpayers. There would be higher rates for upper-income taxpayers in 1987

to make up for lost revenue, as a result of beginning tax cuts in January, rather than July, 1987. The Senate bill had a maximum rate of 27 percent.

2. **Lowering of corporate tax rates.** The first $75,000 of corporate income would be taxed at 15 to 30 percent. The amount above $75,000 would be taxed at 34 percent.
3. **Capital gains.** This income would be taxed at the same rates as regular income, though in 1987 the top rate effectively would be 28 percent, regardless of income. The provisions on capital gains from sale of investments (stocks, bonds, and so on) were closer to those in the Senate bill, rather than in the House measure, in which the top effective rate would be 22 percent.
4. **Minimum tax.** For taxpayers who greatly limit tax liability by gaining income from tax-free preferences, the minimum tax would be retained and redesigned to make it harder for firms to escape taxation. The final provisions were closer to the Senate bill.
5. **Personal exemption.** This exemption would be raised to $2,000 by 1989 for most taxpayers, though it would be effectively phased out for high-income taxpayers. This provision was essentially that of the Senate bill. The House bill had provided a $2,000 exemption for non-itemizers (those who don't itemize deductions) and $1,500 for itemizers.
6. **State and local tax deductions.** Income, real estate, and personal property taxes were to be deductible, while sales taxes would not be subject to deduction. The House bill would have made no changes in the deductibility of state and local taxes; the Senate bill had limited deductions for sales taxes to 60 percent of the amount in excess of state income taxes.
7. **Charitable contributions.** Those persons who itemize deductions would continue to receive full deductions for donations. Nonitemizers would no longer be able to deduct any sums donated for charity. The increased or appreciated value of charitable gifts (e.g., stocks, bonds, other property) would be subject to the minimum tax. The House bill had permitted non-itemizers to deduct donations over $100 but had provided for taxation of the appreciated value of charitable gifts. The Senate bill had eliminated deductions for nonitemizers.
8. **Interest deductions.** Unlimited deductions for mortgages on first and second residences were provided. Limits were placed on other mortgage borrowing. Consumer interest was to be phased out as a deduction. Interest paid on borrowing to produce investment income would be deductible up to the value of the earnings. The final bill was closer to the Senate version, but it deviated from the Reagan plan, which would have capped interest payments above the mortgage interest on a principal residence at $5,000.
9. **Retirement benefits.** IRA contributions were to be limited to those not covered by pension plans or those whose income fell below certain levels specified in the law. Contributions to employer-sponsored (401k) tax-exempt savings plans would be limited to $7,000 annually. Major changes were made

to improve coverage of private pensions and restrict benefits for high-income persons. On the whole, the law followed the provisions set forth in the Senate measure.

10. **Depreciation and investment tax credit.** The investment tax credit was repealed retroactively to January 1, 1986. The system of rapid depreciation found in existing law was largely retained. Larger write-offs for most property would be permitted, but over a longer period of time. The Senate version of the bill was largely adopted.
11. **Business deductions.** Eighty percent (rather than all) of the business meal and entertainment costs would now be deductible. Other employee business expenses would be deductible if they exceeded 2 percent of taxable income. The House deductions for meals and entertainment expenses were accepted by the Senate; the latter body, however, had sought to eliminate most miscellaneous deductions. The administration's plan would have repealed the deduction for entertainment, while limiting business deductions for meals.
12. **Tax-exempt bonds.** The law placed a cap on the use of nongovernment bonds (i.e., those for nongovernment purposes), but excluded charitable organizations from that cap. Some interest would be subject to the minimum tax. The final provisions were a compromise between those found in the House and Senate bills.

Lessons To Be Learned

The 1981 tax reduction and the Tax Reform Act of 1986 demonstrated that tax legislation does not have to be incremental during times of peace. Major changes were made in the rate structure in both bills. The 1986 law in particular significantly altered the provisions dealing with deductions. The former legislation was primarily a tax-reduction measure, while the latter act redistributed the burden by reducing the progressivity of the individual income tax, at the same time eliminating the levies on certain low-income persons and increasing the overall share paid by corporate taxpayers.

The 1981 and 1986 acts had congressional predecessors—bills proposed by members of the House and Senate designed to lower rates and to alter the tax structure. However, it was the persistence of the president and the administration that ultimately led to the adoption of policy proposals that had their genesis in ideas expressed by others.

Both acts were passed after extensive negotiations within Congress and with various interest groups. We have already noted the many compromises that had to be worked out between the House and Senate versions of the 1986 tax reform bill. Although there were only minor amendments to this bill on the floor, hundreds of lobbyists and thousands of citizens expressed opinions on the various changes proposed. Indeed, at one point some observers humorously referred to the bill as the "lobbyists' relief act of 1986." In 1981 Congress added a wide variety of concessions benefiting business to the tax legislation that was being considered.[46]

Although the president was largely responsible for garnering the political support for both pieces of legislation, it is doubtful that he was familiar with many of the details. In fact, David Stockman, his first director of the Office of Management and Budget, suggests that neither Mr. Reagan nor his chief advisers were fully willing to acknowledge the deficit-producing consequences of the 1981 tax reduction.[47] In later years (particularly 1984) Congress had to raise taxes and adopt "revenue enhancers" in order to make up for some of the revenue lost as a result of the reductions that had been mandated.[48]

Tax legislation is inherently complex. Although far-reaching attempts at tax reform had been justified partly on the grounds that the new law would simplify taxes, the final legislation was long—more than 1,000 pages—and complicated. Congress took two years to approve technical changes to the 1986 law, and the IRS did not immediately issue needed regulations to clarify all of the new policies regarding deductions. A survey of IRS answers to questions concerning the new law suggested a year after it was enacted that more than one-third of the responses were incorrect.[49]

Changing the tax structure inevitably means altering the relative share of the cost of running the government that must be borne by various groups. There will be winners and losers or, at least, some persons who win more than others.

SUMMARY

Tax policy is a crucial area of public concern. It involves a distribution of rewards and benefits, costs and penalties for society.

In the United States federal taxes have greatly increased over the years. The growth in revenue is partly a result of increases in population and in the cost of living. However, the introduction of individual and corporate income taxes and payroll taxes for Social Security have significantly enhanced the moneys secured by the national government.

There are many actors involved in the making of tax policy. Congress has the power to tax, and the House Ways and Means and Senate Finance committees unquestionably play an important role in fashioning legislation. We have also noted that the president, some of his chief political and economic advisers, bureaucrats in the executive branch, committee staff members, and interest groups participate in shaping tax law.

Although policy is often made incrementally, it is possible for major changes to be made during peacetime. The 1981 and 1986 tax legislation illustrate what can be done when a persistent president coaxes Congress to alter fundamental provisions of tax law.

Of course, major changes in the tax code have long-term consequences. As we will see when we examine spending policy, large-scale cuts in revenue influence expenditures and may help determine how much the government must borrow.

NOTES

[1]John F. Witte, "A Long View of Tax Reform", *National Tax Journal*, vol. 39, no. 3 (September 1986), 256.

[2]*Pollock* v. *Farmers' Loan and Trust Co.*, 158 U.S. 601 (1895).

[3]John F. Witte, *The Politics and Development of the Federal Income Tax* (Madison: University of Wisconsin Press, 1985), pp. 67–75.

[4]For a discussion of the income tax during the World War I and the interwar years, see Witte, *The Politics and Development of the Federal Income Tax*, pp. 79–109.

[5]Stanley S. Surrey, "How Special Tax Provisions Get Enacted," in Raymond E. Wolfinger, ed., *Readings in American Political Behavior* (2nd ed.; Englewood Cliffs, NJ: Prentice Hall, 1970), pp. 257–265.

[6]Although the enforcement and rule-making powers of the IRS are great, the IRS can be checked by the courts. The U.S. Tax Court in particular hears many cases arising from taxpayer challenges to IRS decisions.

[7]In 1985, for example, a married couple with two dependents with an adjusted gross income of $75,000 had a marginal tax rate (the percentage of the first additional dollar of income that would be paid in income taxes) of 42 percent. After exclusions, its true or effective rate was 23.5 percent. U.S. Bureau of the Census, *Statistical Abstract of the United States: 1986* (106th ed.), Washington, DC, 1985, p. 319.

[8]Walter J. Blum and Harry Kalven, Jr., *The Uneasy Case for Progressive Taxation* (Chicago: University of Chicago Press, 1953), pp. 14–28. Also see Witte, *The Politics and Development of the Federal Income Tax*, pp. 27–64.

[9]For an analysis of the value-added tax, see Wayne R. Thirsk, "The Value-Added Tax in Canada: Saviour or Siren Song?" *Canadian Public Policy*, vol. 12, no. 3 (September 1987), 259–283.

[10]John Maynard Keynes, *The General Theory of Employment, Interest, and Money* (New York: Harcourt, 1936).

[11]For a critical discussion of Keynesian ideas, see Henry Hazlitt, ed., *The Critics of Keynesian Economics* (New York: D. Van Nostrand, 1960).

[12]Jude Wanniski, *The Way the World Works: How Economies Fail—and Succeed* (New York: Basic Books, 1978); and Gene C. Uselton, "The Case for Reaganomics," *Texas Business Review*, vol. 56 (May–June 1982), 105–109.

[13]David A. Stockman, *The Triumph of Politics: How the Reagan Revolution Failed* (New York: Harper & Row, Pub., 1986), pp. 98–99, 229–268.

[14]*Ibid.*, pp. 98, 330, 340; Ray Marshall, "The Case Against Reaganomics," *Texas Business Review*, vol. 56 (May–June 1982), 110–117.

[15]For a discussion of "tax expenditures" (i.e., tax breaks) for business, see Ira C. Magaziner and Robert B. Reich, *Minding America's Business: The Decline*

and Rise of the American Economy (New York: Law and Business, 1982), pp. 243–244.

[16] "The Making of a Miracle," *Time* (August 25, 1986), p. 15.

[17]One of the reasons for opposition to the administration's original tax-reform plan, which was introduced at the end of 1984, was that it reduced or eliminated many incentives for people to invest money or give generously to charities. It would also tax life- and health-insurance benefits provided to workers by employers. "Up Go the Trial Balloons," *Time* (December 10, 1984), pp. 20–24.

[18] "Congress Enacts President Reagan's Tax Plan," in *Congressional Quarterly Almanac: 1981* (Washington, DC: Congressional Quarterly, 1982), p. 91.

[19]*Ibid.*, p. 95.

[20]*Ibid.*, p. 92.

[21]*Ibid.*, pp. 97–98.

[22]*Ibid.*, p. 98.

[23]*Ibid.*, pp. 98–99.

[24]*Ibid.*, pp. 100–102.

[25]*Ibid.*, p. 103.

[26]*Ibid.*

[27]*Ibid.*, p. 92.

[28]John F. Kelly, Jr., "Legislative History of the Tax Reform Act of 1986," in *The Tax Reform Act of 1986: Detailed Analysis*, vol. 2, ed. Leonard L. Silverstein (Washington, DC: Tax Management Inc, 1987), p. ix; and "Congress Enacts Sweeping Overhaul of Tax Law," in *Congressional Quarterly Almanac 1986* (Washington, DC: Congressional Quarterly, Inc., 1987), p. 491.

[29]"The State of the Union Address," January 25, 1984, *Weekly Compilation of Presidential Documents*, vol. 20, no. 4, p. 90.

[30]Kelly, p. ix.

[31]David E. Rosenbaum, "Reagan Gets Treasury Plan Calling for Rise in Corporate Burden," *New York Times*, November 27, 1984, pp. 1, 48; and Jeff Nesbit, "Tax Reform Could Cripple Updating of Steel Industry," *Akron Beacon Journal*, December 2, 1984, p. A4.

[32]Kelly, p. ix.

[33]*Ibid.*

[34]*Ibid.* See also, "President Proposes Federal Tax Reform," *Congressional Quarterly Almanac: 1985* (Washington, DC: Congressional Quarterly, 1986), pp. 20D–22D.

[35]Kelly, p. x.

[36]*Ibid.*

[37]*Ibid.*

[38]*Ibid*; and "Congress Enacts Sweeping Overhaul of Tax Law," p. 506.

[39]"Congress Enacts Sweeping Overhaul of Tax Law," pp. 492–493.

[40]Jeffrey H. Birnbaum and Alan S. Murray, *Showdown at Gucci Gulch: Lawmakers, Lobbyists, and the Unlikely Triumph of Tax Reform* (New York: Random House, 1987), pp. 177–179.

[41]Kelly, p. x.

[42]*Ibid.*, pp. x–xi.

[43]*Ibid.*, p. xi.

[44]*Ibid.*

[45]"Congress Enacts Sweeping Overhaul of Tax Law," pp. 492–493.

[46]Stockman, pp. 231–232, 248–251, 260–261, 267–268; and "Christmastime on Capitol Hill," *Time* (July 27, 1981), p. 25. Also see Birnbaum and Murray, p. 177.

[47]Stockman, pp. 269–326.

[48] "Spending Cuts, Tax Increases," *Congressional Quarterly Almanac: 1984* (Washington, DC: Congressional Quarterly, 1985), pp. 144–155.

[49]Robert Pear, "Errors Found in a Third of Replies by IRS to Phoned Tax Questions," *New York Times*, February 23, 1988, pp. A1, D9.

CHAPTER FIVE

Monetary Policy

Money is, with propriety, considered as the vital principle of the body politic; as that which sustains its life and motion and enables it to perform its most essential functions.[1]

Alexander Hamilton

THE FEDERAL RESERVE SYSTEM

About 8 times each year, the 12 members of the Open Market Committee of the Federal Reserve System meet to set goals for the expansion of the money supply in the United States. The decisions they reach help to determine how much businesses will expand, prices will rise, and employment will grow or diminish. They act without having to consult the president and without clear guidelines from Congress. How did a group of nonelected officials in our central bank acquire such power, and through what mechanisms do they exercise control over the credit available in our economy?

The answers to these questions are at once both simple and complicated. The Federal Reserve system was created in 1913 during the administration of Woodrow Wilson. Its primary purpose was to safeguard the banking system against panics such as those that occurred in the late nineteenth century and in 1907, when many institutions failed and depositors suffered severe losses. As the central bank for the United States, the Federal Reserve Bank, often referred to simply as the Fed, was charged with providing an elastic currency and serving as a lender of last resort to the nation's banks.[2]

Its complex organization reflects the fears of excessive concentration of banking power and the need for regional interests to be represented in the decision-making process. The Federal Reserve system consists of several components, the most important of which are the Board of Governors, the 12 District Reserve Banks and their branch offices, and the Federal Open Market Committee (FOMC) (See Figure 5–1). By law, all nationally chartered commercial banks and certain state-chartered institutions that meet standards established by the Fed are part of the Federal Reserve System.

The Board of Governors consists of 7 members appointed for 14 years by the president, subject to confirmation by the Senate. The person selected by the president as chairman of the Board of Governors serves in that capacity for a 4-year term, although he may be reappointed. The terms of the governors are staggered, one expiring every 2 years.

The board is responsible for the overall operations of the Fed. It determines broad monetary, credit, and operating policies for the system and formulates the rules and regulations for carrying out the purposes of the Federal Reserve Act. Its duties include monitoring credit conditions, supervising the Federal Reserve District Banks and member banks, and helping to implement certain consumer credit protection laws.

There are Federal Reserve Banks in 12 major financial centers: Boston, New York, Philadelphia, Cleveland, Richmond, Atlanta, Chicago, St. Louis, Minneapolis, Kansas City, Dallas, and San Francisco. There are 25 branch banks in other important commercial cities.

Each reserve bank has a nine-member Board of Directors; three are class A directors elected by member banks, while the three class B directors, who are also elected by the member banks, must be actively engaged in their districts in commerce, agriculture, or industry, and cannot be officers, directors, or employees of any bank. The three class C directors, who cannot be officers, directors, employees, or stockholders of any bank, are appointed by the Board of Governors. The Board of Governors appoints a class C director as chairman of the Board of Directors of the reserve bank. The president and first vice-president of each reserve bank are appointed by the Board of Directors, subject to approval by the Board of Governors.

The reserve banks receive the reserve deposits of depository institutions. They can lend money or extend credit to both member and nonmember banks.

The Federal Open Market Committee is made up of the Board of Governors and five of the presidents of the reserve banks, one of whom is always the president of the Federal Reserve Bank of New York. The other four presidents rotate annually.

The committee meets frequently in Washington and establishes regulations for the purchases and sales of securities, principally obligations of the United States government and federal agencies, in the open market. These transactions are executed by the Federal Reserve Bank of New York. They are designed to expand or contract the supply of money as needed for long-term economic growth and to meet temporary demands for money and credit. The FOMC also directs the Federal Reserve Bank of New York to undertake transactions in foreign currencies for the Federal Reserve System Open Market Account in order to safeguard the value of the dollar in international markets and to facilitate growth in liquidity to meet the needs of the expanding global economy.

There are 3 advisory bodies, which meet with the Board of Governors periodically. The Federal Advisory Council, composed of 12 members, 1 from each Federal Reserve district, is selected by the various Boards of Directors of the reserve banks. It confers with the Board of Governors on general business conditions. The Consumer Advisory Council, established by Congress at the suggestion of the Board of Governors in 1976, is made up of 30 members and discusses problems related to consumer credit protection. The Thrift Institutions Advisory Council, established by the board in 1980, is composed of representatives from savings and loans, mutual savings banks, and credit unions. It meets with the Board of Governors to discuss developments concerning thrift institutions, the housing industry and mortgage finance, and related regulatory matters.

The powers of the Fed are extensive. It serves through the reserve banks as a clearinghouse and collecting agent for depository institutions in the handling of checks and other instruments. The reserve banks also issue Federal Reserve notes, which make up most of the money in circulation. They act as depositories and fiscal agents of the United States government and help to issue and redeem federal securities.

The Board of Governors has broad regulatory power over the banks that are members of the system, and it regulates disclosure of terms of credit by various lenders. The board also regulates the use of margin credit in the purchase of stocks and other securities. In practice, the board can effectively influence the district banks. It frequently recommends a choice for president of the Federal Reserve Bank to the directors, who usually follow its suggestions. It also sets the salary of the president and reviews the budget of each Federal Reserve Bank.

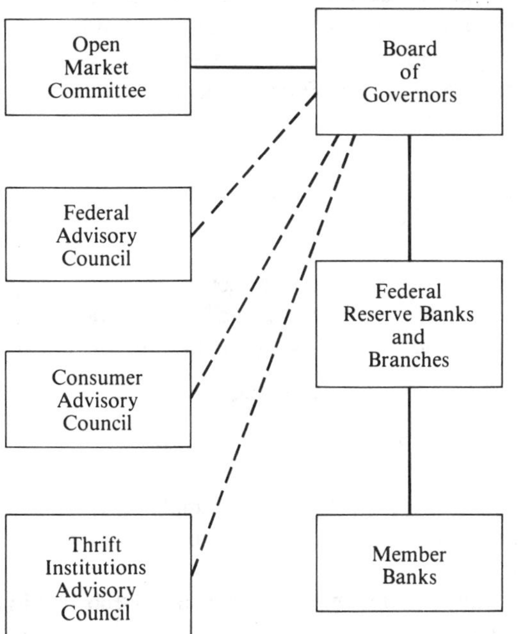

Figure 5–1 The Federal Reserve system.

The most important powers of the Federal Reserve System, however, are those that are exercised over the money supply. There are three major ways in which the Fed can influence the availability of money and the rates of interest that people must pay when they need credit. The Board of Governors can raise or lower **reserve requirements**—the amount of funds that banks and other depository institutions must deposit with the local Federal Reserve Bank or set aside as vault cash, unavailable to lend to businesses and consumers. In consultation with the Federal Reserve Banks, it can raise or lower the **discount rates**—the rate of interest charged to depository institutions that need to borrow from the system. Through the FOMC, the Fed can buy or sell United States government securities.

Reserve requirements are not often used to control the supply of money in our country, although they do indirectly control the cost of money by making credit more or less available. The discount rates could influence the availability of money and its cost, but most institutions do not borrow heavily from the Fed, and indeed there are penalties for those that must do so. The discount rate determines the cost of money more than its availability, because an institution will of necessity lend money at a higher rate than it must pay to borrow funds. Most borrowing by banks is done to obtain funds over night. The interest they pay, the federal funds rate, is paid by borrowing banks to those that lend the money because they have excess funds on hand. The federal funds rate is not directly set by the Federal Reserve system and may fluctuate from day to day.

The transactions of the FOMC are unquestionably the most important way for the Fed to influence the supply of money. If the committee wishes to contract the money supply, it sells United States government obligations and federal agency securities on the open market. Thus, it secures money that it can hold in reserve. When it wishes to expand the money supply, it purchases government securities from the banks. The banks receive a credit at their Federal Reserve Bank, which can then be lent to the public.[3]

PROBLEMS IN MAKING MONETARY POLICY

There are many problems associated with the making of monetary policy. Among the most important are those that concern the ability of the Federal Reserve system to control the money supply, the discretion of the Fed, and the proper mix of monetary and fiscal policies.

Controlling the Money Supply

As we noted previously, the Fed can seek to control the supply of money by altering the reserve requirements, setting the discount rates, and buying and selling government securities. Through these actions the Fed particularly tries to influence the size of M1—the amount of currency in circulation and the sums deposited in checking accounts and traveler's checks.

However, the supply of money is more than M1. Economists and the members of the Board of Governors have recognized as well the importance of small-denomination time deposits, savings deposits, money market accounts, noninstitutional money market mutual fund shares, overnight repurchase agreements, and the like. Together with the categories of money and deposits in M1, these components are part of M2. An even larger monetary aggregate, M3, includes the categories in M1 and M2 plus large-denomination time deposits (over $100,000), money market mutual fund balances for institutions, long-term repurchase agreements, and so on. M2 and M3 are several times larger than the more limited money measure, M1.[4]

In recent years the task of controlling the money supply has become much more difficult for several reasons. First, there has been a proliferation of nonbank institutions that accept deposits, such as brokerage houses that have established special accounts and mutual funds of all kinds. Second, the widespread use of credit cards issued by banks, thrift institutions, and brokers makes "plastic money" expandable and difficult to regulate. Third, Eurodollars—dollars invested in banks abroad by individuals and businesses—are largely beyond the power of any federal agency to control. International flows of capital on a large scale are facts of modern economic life. In the absence of rigid currency and investment regulation, which would probably require multinational cooperation to implement, it is nearly impossible to control the expansion and contraction of money as it enters or leaves the United States.[5]

Federal Reserve Discretion

For the most part, the Board of Governors and the FOMC have set goals for the expansion and contraction of the money supply without following any rigid rules. They have instead considered a variety of changing economic conditions—levels of unemployment and production, inflation rates, and so on—and have tried to alter the money supply accordingly.[6] In essence, there has been an element of fine tuning.

Some economists have argued that the current system gives the Fed too much power. It does not have to take direction from the elected branches of government, unlike the central banks of most democratic nations, and it lacks the skill and wisdom to change the money supply frequently in response to modifications of the economic environment. Milton Friedman, one of the leading critics of Federal Reserve policy, has argued for a monetarist approach, one that would provide fairly constant growth in the money supply every year. Friedman believes that an annual increase in the money supply of approximately 3 to 5 percent would be sufficient to allow for economic growth without stimulating inflationary pressures.[7]

Those who favor a significant measure of independence for the Fed argue that it must be free from political pressure when making decisions about monetary policy. They fear that partisan influences would lead to questionable decisions if the president and Congress could directly determine the expansion or contraction of money.[8]

Some recent studies of the Federal Reserve system suggest that the independence of that body has been exaggerated. Although congressional interest in the Federal Reserve has been only intermittent and rarely leads to strong and decisive action, the Fed usually goes along with the wishes of the administration. Presidents normally get what they want from the central bank.[9]

The Fed also has to deal with other constituencies, particularly the community of bankers and investment firm executives, groups whose concerns are likely to be given respectful attention. Persons with unorthodox economic ideas have practically no chance of being nominated for membership on the Board of Governors, and only those who are bankers or financial economists are generally appointed to that body. Moreover, staff economists who work for the Federal Reserve system frequently leave the agency to work for banks and other financial institutions. Thus, it is not surprising that the Fed often seems to have a close relationship, if not an identity of interests, with important segments of the financial community.[10]

Monetary and Fiscal Policy

Monetarists believe that the supply of money is the key determinant of economic growth and inflation. An adequate money supply is necessary to provide the capital for new investment and the creation of jobs. Excessive growth of money in circulation will lead to inflation; inadequate growth may lead to recession.[11]

Keynesian economists, as we noted in an earlier chapter, emphasize fiscal policy as the stimulus and brake on the economy. Taxation and spending become the major means for maintaining stable prices and preventing sharp downturns in demand and production.

Generally speaking, Democrats have been more inclined to use fiscal policy to promote economic stability and prosperity, while Republicans have been more likely to use monetary policy. These interparty differences have been somewhat blurred in recent years as a result of support for supply-side economics among some Republicans. Supply-side economists, of course, have focused on tax rates, urging their reduction to more generally acceptable levels in order to stimulate greater productivity. Supply-siders have not endorsed massive deficits, but they do not seem adverse to some short-run deficit spending if that will promote better economic conditions.[12]

Policy-makers are not limited to using only one tool to promote price stability and relatively high levels of production and employment. Both fiscal and monetary policy can be employed. The question often becomes one of finding the appropriate mix and deciding how to use each policy component in order to promote desired objectives.

An increase in taxes can reduce demand and curb inflationary pressures; it can also serve as a catalyst for recession, particularly if government surpluses are generated at a time of falling production in the private sector. Reducing the supply of money or increasing its cost may help to cool down an overheated economy, but a lessening of credit may also prove ruinous to small businesses, that need capital for expansion and low-interest loans for consumers who wish to make sizable purchases. As we will see in the next section, there are winners and losers whenever monetary policy is made.

THE FED UNDER PAUL VOLCKER

In 1979, inflation as measured by the consumer price index (CPI) exceeded 12 percent. Wall Street investors were worried as they saw the value of their investments rapidly decline. The White House was also concerned. President Jimmy Carter appointed G. William Miller, who was chairman of the Board of Governors, to be the new secretary of the Treasury, replacing Michael Blumenthal. Who would fill Miller's post?

One person whose name was recommended to the president was Paul Adolph Volcker. Volcker, who had received training in economics and public administration, was president of the New York Federal Reserve Bank. Volcker, a Democrat, was a conservative and somewhat austere individual, who insisted that the Fed's independence be respected.[13]

He was offered the post as chairman of the Board of Governors after A. W. Clausen, president of the Bank of America, declined the position. The president decided to select Volcker as Fed chairman, despite concerns about whether he would cooperate sufficiently with the administration and after a warning from Bert Lance, Carter's friend and political adviser, not to appoint him.

A key White House staff member said that "Volcker was selected because he was the candidate of Wall Street."[14] The financial community saw him as an individual who could stem the rapid rise in prices that threatened the stock market.

In October 1979, two months after his appointment as chairman of the Board of Governors, Volcker called a Saturday evening news conference and announced a plan to defeat inflation. He said that money-supply growth would be strictly limited, even if interest rates greatly increased. It took over two years, a 20.5 percent prime rate (the rate of interest charged by banks to their best business customers), and the onset of a major recession to bring inflation under control.[15]

For most of his first three years in office, Volcker pursued his tight money policies vigorously. By word and deed, he did his best to restrict the supply of money. A mixture of discount-rate adjustments, credit controls,[16] and Open Market transactions were all used to limit monetary growth.

Volcker's policies often came under attack. Within the Board of Governors, he faced opposition from those members who feared excessively high interest rates and their effects on business and agriculture. Nancy Teeters, a liberal Democrat also appointed by President Carter, was one of his more persistent critics. By the end of his second term, he faced increased opposition from Reagan appointees as well.[17]

Some members of Congress contended that his policies were harmful and potentially ruinous to small businesspeople and farmers. For example, Senator

Robert Byrd, the Democratic floor leader, and 31 other cosponsors tried in 1982 to push through legislation to force the Fed to reduce interest rates. Before interest rates began to tumble later in the year, the Senate majority leader, Howard Baker, privately joined in the criticism of Volcker. Interestingly, Congressman Jack Kemp of New York, a Republican supply-sider, was also critical of Volcker and supported measures to limit the discretion of the Fed.[18]

Within the Reagan administration, supply-siders criticized his restrictive moves. Under-Secretary of the Treasury Paul Craig Roberts attacked him as a saboteur of Reaganomics. Donald Regan, secretary of the Treasury and later White House chief of staff, was critical of his antiexpansionary views and support for high interest rates. James Baker, who later became secretary of the Treasury, was concerned about the detrimental economic and political effects of the Fed's policies.[19]

Despite his critics, Volcker was reappointed in 1983 by President Reagan to serve a second term as head of the Federal Reserve system. During his eight years in office, he became one of the major policy-makers in the United States and, arguably, as some of the commentators on the Fed have suggested, the second most powerful man in the government.

Why was Paul Volcker able to exercise such influence over the economy? Certain institutional and personal characteristics help to explain why the Fed chairman exerted great control over the economic life of the nation.

Although the chairperson of the Board of Governors has only one vote when monetary policy questions are decided, by tradition he has been the primary spokesman for, and leader of, that body. Moreover, he has overall power to supervise and direct the staff employed by the board.[20]

Volcker demonstrated an understanding of, and a capability to use, the resources at his disposal. His background as an economist may not have differentiated him from most of the other governors, but his service as president of the New York Federal Reserve Bank made him an important insider.

Although he was a nominal Democrat, Volcker was not widely viewed as a partisan. Indeed, most of his career in government service had been under Republican administrations. He was skillful at forming coalitions within the board to secure support for his policy preferences.[21]

Volcker's views concerning the necessity of combatting inflation by restricting growth in the money supply did not change, but he was enough of a pragmatist to alter his tactics to take into account new environmental conditions. For example, he let interest rates drop in 1982, when a world recession came close to forcing Mexico to default on its debt. When inflation rates dropped substantially in 1986, he allowed money growth to surge to its highest levels in the postwar period. In 1987, as inflation showed signs of picking up again, the Fed began to limit credit.[22]

The Fed chairman was adept at managing crises. He prevented the debt situation in major Third World nations such as Mexico and Brazil from erupting into chaos. In 1984, Volcker successfully managed a near panic caused by the collapse of Continental Illinois National Bank and Trust Company. He arranged for short-term loans to the bank and assisted in the federal takeover of the foundering institution.[23]

Two common criticisms of Volcker's leadership were that he dealt more with the symptoms of problems than with their underlying causes, and that he was difficult to get along with. His handling of the foreign debt situation and the Continental Illinois failure did nothing to change the basic problems faced by Third World countries or by American banks. He was better at coming up with *ad hoc* resolutions for crises than at finding fundamental solutions. He eschewed long-term planning, because he believed that such planning involved only abstractions.[24]

His aloof nature made it hard for people to deal with him. He did little to maintain contact with key officials in the Reagan administration, and he was not particularly close to Jimmy Carter, who had appointed him.[25]

One of the most serious criticisms of his policies was that he caused great hardship in the country by forcing up interest rates and bringing on the worst economic downtown since the Great Depression. At the height of the recession in 1982, more than one of ten Americans was out of work. There were more business failures than there had been in several decades.[26] Clearly, in order to lower inflation, the interests of many Americans were sacrificed. Although the stock market began a period of significant growth, it was nevertheless true that there were real losers in the war to limit price increases.

Volcker's defenders suggest that he set a good example for his successors who would have to handle inflation. Volcker himself has said that the sacrifices endured at the start of the decade helped to bring about the sustained expansion that we later experienced, an economic growth accompanied by relatively little inflation.[27]

SUMMARY

We have seen that the Federal Reserve system is the main institution that makes American monetary policy. It can influence the growth of the money supply in several ways: by changing the reserve requirements of banks, by altering the discount rates, and by purchasing or selling government securities on the open market.

Among the major problems concerning the making of monetary policy are those that deal with the ability of the Fed to control the money supply, the degree of discretion of the Federal Reserve system, and the appropriate mix of monetary and fiscal components.

When decisions are made on the supply of money and the availability of credit, there are winners and losers. Some businesses and consumers clearly need low-interest loans more than others.

We previously noted that the Federal Reserve system is involved in some regulatory activities. In the next chapter we will examine in more detail the arguments for and against economic regulation, as well as the role of regulatory agencies.

NOTES

[1]Alexander Hamilton, "Federalist No. 30," in Alexander Hamilton, James Madison, and John Jay, *The Federalist Papers* (New York: New American Library of World Literature, 1961), p. 188.

[2]Frederic S. Mishkin, *The Economics of Money, Banking, and Financial Markets* (2d ed.; Glenview, Il: Scott, Foresman, 1989), p. 333.

[3]*Ibid.*, pp. 334–341; *The United States Government Manual, 1988/89* (Washington, DC: Office of the Federal Register, 1988), pp. 562–569; and Thibaut De Saint Phalle, *The Federal Reserve: An Intentional Mystery* (New York: Praeger, 1985), pp. 3–14.

[4]Mishkin, pp. 31–33.

[5]Jonathan Rowe, "The Cult of M1," *The Washington Monthly* (November 1983), 14–22.

[6]Mishkin, pp. 386–408; and Saint Phalle, pp. 87–129.

[7]Michael D. Reagan, "The Political Structure of the Federal Reserve System," *American Political Science Review*, 55 (March 1961), 64–76; Milton Friedman, "The Case for Overhauling the Federal Reserve," *Challenge*, 28 (July–August 1985), 4–12; George P. Brockway, "A Requiem for Monetarism," *The New Leader*, 69 (October 6, 1986), 13–15; and Milton Friedman and Rose Friedman, *Free to Choose: A Personal Statement* (New York: Avon, 1981), pp. 255, 295–296.

[8]Mishkin, pp. 346–347.

[9]Nathaniel Beck, "Presidential Influence on the Federal Reserve in the 1970s," *American Journal of Political Science*, 26 (August 1982), 415–445; and John T. Woolley, *Monetary Politics: The Federal Reserve and the Politics of Monetary Policy* (New York: Cambridge University Press, 1984), pp. 109, 152–153.

[10]William Greider, *Secrets of the Temple: How the Federal Reserve Runs the Country* (New York: Simon & Schuster, 1987), pp. 72–73.

[11]Leonard Silk, *The Economists* (New York: Avon, 1978), pp. 73–75.

[12]For a discussion of some of the attitudes of supply-siders concerning deficits, see David A. Stockman, *The Triumph of Politics: Why the Reagan Revolution Failed* (New York: Harper & Row, Pub.,1986), pp. 52–54, 309, 322.

[13] Greider, pp. 45–46.

[14]*Ibid.*, p. 47

[15]"America's Money Master," *Newsweek* (February 24, 1986), 46–53.

[16]Credit controls were only used temporarily as part of a bargain with President Carter in 1980 to reduce the budget and show that the administration was taking steps to fight inflation. Greider, pp. 182–186; and Adam Smith, "The Volcker Legacy," *Esquire* (August 1988), 72–73.

[17]Greider, pp. 465–469, 568, 612, 677–679.

[18]*Ibid.*, pp. 474–475, 515, 602, 607–608.

[19]*Ibid.*, pp. 541, 555–556.

[20]Jack H. Knott, "The Fed Chairman as a Political Executive," *Administration and Society*, 18 (August 1986), 197–231.

[21]"America's Money Master," p. 47; Smith, pp. 71–73; and Greider, pp. 68, 78.

[22]Blanca Riemer, "The Lesson of Paul Volcker: Inflation Can Be Beaten," *Business Week* (June 15, 1987), 30.

[23]*Ibid*; and Greider, pp. 630–631.

[24]Riemer; "Advice from Mr. Chairman," *Time* (January 23, 1989), 50; and David Fand, "Paul Volcker's Legacy," *Policy Review*, no. 34 (Fall 1985), 58–63.

[25]Riemer; and "Advice from Mr. Chairman," pp. 49–50.

[26]Greider, pp. 450–463, 530; and Jonathan Alter, "Defrocking the Fed," *The Washington Monthly* (June 1982), 12–21.

[27]"America's Money Master;" p. 51; and "Advice from Mr. Chairman," p. 49.

CHAPTER SIX

Economic Regulation

> The state is completely discharged from a duty, in attempting to perform which it must always be exposed to innumerable delusions, and for the proper performance of which no human wisdom or knowledge could ever be sufficient: the impossible task of superintending the industry of private people, and of directing it towards the employments most suitable to the interest of the society.[1]
>
> *Adam Smith*

> There can be no delusion more fatal to the nation, than the delusion that the standard of profits, of business prosperity, is sufficient in judging any business or political question—from rate legislation to municipal government. Business success, whether for the individual or for the nation, is a good thing only so far as it is accompanied by and develops a high standard of conduct—honor, integrity, civic courage.[2]
>
> *Theodore Roosevelt*

GOVERNMENT REGULATION

History of Federal Regulation

In 1776, the year in which the Declaration of Independence was adopted by the Continental Congress in Philadelphia, Adam Smith, a professor at the University of Glasgow, wrote a work that was to alter economic thought in much of the western world. *The Wealth of Nations* argued that the pursuit of self-interest, rather than government edicts, could best help people meet their material needs and secure their happiness. The marketplace would serve as the mechanism for merchants and manufacturers to decide on the goods they produced and the prices they charged. Decisions would be made in response to consumer demand. The role of the state was limited. It had the responsibility of protecting the country from invasion, administering justice, and building and maintaining useful public works that could not be profitably erected or maintained by individuals.

Smith advocated the use of competition to ensure that the market was kept free. However, the government's economic role was more that of an enabler than a regulator. On the whole, he believed that government should adopt a laissez faire stance vis-à-vis business; that is, government should leave business alone rather than seek to supervise and aid it. Smith was the intellectual father of classical capitalism.[3]

Smith's ideas were very different from the mercantilist views of most eighteenth-century economists and political decision-makers. Mercantilism represented mainly the interests of established merchants of the great European powers. It supported state direction of the economy. Mercantilism assumed that gold and silver represented real wealth, and therefore a nation must secure a large store of bullion. In order to do so it must encourage trade with other countries, so that it could export goods and acquire more gold and silver from them. To maintain a favorable balance of trade, restrictive practices were adopted, such as giving a monopoly of the carrying trade to one's own merchant marine and limiting colonies to the provision of raw materials. Monopoly was seen as the most efficient means of promoting trade and accumulating bullion.[4] In short, mercantilism saw a significant economic role for government and was anticompetitive in its thrust.

In the early years of our country's history most political leaders tended to favor a limited role for government in regulating the economy. Among the economic grievances of the colonists who rebelled against British rule were the restrictions that the mother country placed on trade, navigation, and manufacturing. American merchants were restricted in their ability to trade with colonies or states that were not part of the British Empire. Goods had to be carried in British flag ships. Factories that competed with British producers were discouraged. Monopolies for the sale of certain items, such as tea, were granted by the royal government.[5] It is little wonder that economic freedom was generally seen as a liberating force to expand opportunity for the free population.

Of course, mercantilist ideas did not evaporate overnight. Alexander Hamilton, the first secretary of the Treasury, wanted to strengthen the American economy by encouraging manufacturing. This he proposed to do by granting bounties to domestic manufacturers and imposing tariffs on imported goods to protect nascent industries.[6]

Thomas Jefferson, Albert Gallatin, and Henry Clay were among the members of the executive and legislative branches who favored using federal funds to open up the West. Although their proposals generally included land purchases and internal improvements (roads, harbors, and so on) rather than monopolies and highly restrictive trade practices, it is nevertheless true that they wanted to use public resources to direct economic development in a particular part of the country.[7]

The nineteenth century saw the growth of an intricate system of canals and railroads. Much of that new system of transportation was aided or built with public funds. Although state governments provided much of the original capital for the construction of canals and railways, federal land grants and moneys made possible the building of the transcontinental railroad.[8]

While the public sector was generous in subsidizing the growth of the railroad industry, there was little attempt at national regulation until the 1880s. In 1887, Congress passed the Act to Regulate Commerce, which established the Interstate Commerce Commission. This legislation was passed partly in response to discriminatory rate practices employed by many railroads. It also was a response to the desire of the railroad industry to be subject to national regulation rather than the rules and laws of many states. The act provided that all charges must be reasonable and just, prohibited discrimination, prohibited higher charges for short hauls than for long hauls, forbade pooling of the freight of competing railroads, required public notice of rates, and set up a commission to investigate violations of the law. Although the Interstate Commerce Commission could collect statistics, hear complaints and render decisions in cases brought before it, the enforcement of the decisions was obtained through the courts. Judicial interpretation of the act weakened the powers of the commission, so that it became a body with little power beyond that of filing reports and issuing protests.[9]

At the same time the railroads first came under national regulation, there were growing demands for other rules to govern the power of the giant companies that were being created as the United States became a great industrial power. Trusts—monopolies operating over large areas or the entire nation—had been established in a variety of industries, including oil, sugar, and tobacco.

To control these monopolies, Congress passed the Sherman Anti-Trust Act in 1890. The Sherman Act made it illegal to engage in any contract, combination, or conspiracy in restraint of interstate or foreign commerce. Antitrust legislation was not effectively enforced until the administration of Theodore Roosevelt.[10]

During the period of Theodore Roosevelt's presidency, the powers of the government to prosecute the railroads were also strengthened through the passage of the Elkins Act of 1903. In 1906 the Hepburn Act enlarged the powers of the Interstate Commerce Commission and extended detailed government supervision over the common carriers of the country, including express and sleeping car trains, pipeline companies, switching and terminal facilities, and the railroads.[11]

In 1910 the Mann-Elkins Act brought express, telegraph, telephone, and cable companies under the control of the Interstate Commerce Commission. The Commission was also given the power to suspend all proposed increases in rates until it could hold hearings and determine whether the increases were reasonable.[12]

During the Wilson administration, two major laws pertaining to trusts were passed. A Federal Trade Commission was created in 1914 to administer antitrust legislation and prevent unfair competition. It was given power to issue "cease and desist" orders to prevent misbranding of goods, false advertising, and price discrimination.[13]

The Clayton Anti-Trust Act, also passed in 1914, specifically defined certain unfair practices. These practices included price discrimination among various purchasers, exclusive dealer contracts, one corporation's holding the stock of another if this would substantially lessen competition, interlocking directorates, and relationships between railroads and construction companies.[14]

Another great period of regulation occurred during the 1930s and resulted from the uncertainties of the Great Depression and the perceived inefficiencies and inequities of the marketplace. During Franklin Roosevelt's administration, Congress agreed for a time to suspend antitrust regulations. The National Industrial Recovery Act (NRA), passed in 1933, mandated the formation of planning boards for certain critical areas of the economy. The boards, with business and labor representation, were authorized to set output goals, prices, and wages for the industry. The NRA was declared unconstitutional in 1935,[15] but other regulatory legislation was also enacted.

Congress passed laws to extend the rights of workers. The National Labor Relations Act, passed in 1935, set up a three-person board to prevent employers from engaging in unfair labor practices (such as using labor spies, employing strikebreakers, circulating propaganda against unions that would cause workers to fear the loss of their jobs, and discharging employees for union activities) and to conduct elections among employees to determine which union should represent them in bargaining with management. The Fair Labor Standards Act of 1938 established the basic 40-hour work week and required payment of a minimum wage to most industrial workers.[16]

Legislation was passed to provide price supports to farmers. At the same time, production quotas were established to discourage surpluses. After the Supreme Court declared the Agricultural Adjustment Act unconstitutional in 1936, Congress enacted the Soil Conservation and Domestic Allotment Act, which continued crop regulation.[17]

The banking and investment industries were altered in several ways. The powers of the Federal Reserve System were strengthened. Federal insurance for banks and thrift institutions was provided. Under the Glass-Steagall Act of 1933, commercial banks were prohibited from engaging in the underwriting and dealing of corporate securities. The Securities and Exchange Commission was created to regulate the sale of stocks and bonds.[18]

The Second World War saw a great growth in the regulatory powers of the federal government. Even during World War I the national government had taken over the railroads, and attempts were made to control the distribution of food and other scarce resources. During World War II the government made widespread use of rationing and wage and price controls, and even tried to limit the movement of workers from one place of business to another.[19]

In the years following the war, many of the controls were ended or relaxed. Nevertheless, the regulatory role of the federal government continued. The Employment Act of 1946 made it a goal of the United States government "... to promote maximum employment, production and purchasing power," thus making the national authorities guarantors of prosperity as well as regulators.[20] Congress restrained labor unions by passing the Taft-Hartley Act, which permitted the enjoining of strikes that threatened the safety or economic welfare of the nation and allowed states to pass "right to work" laws, outlawing compulsory union membership as a condition of employment.[21]

In the 1960s and 1970s the country became increasingly concerned with consumer safety and environmental issues. In 1970 the Occupational Safety and Health Act created the Occupational Safety and Health Administration to inspect plants and protect worker safety. President Nixon established the Environmental Protection Agency in 1971 through an executive order to enforce pollution-control regulations. In 1973 the Consumer Product Safety Commission was created to protect American consumers.[22]

Even as new regulatory bodies were being set up, a countertrend was beginning to develop. Starting with the Nixon and Ford administrations and continuing through the Carter and Reagan presidencies, there was a movement to reduce regulatory controls and the paperwork accompanying government efforts at regulation. For example, controls on the price of domestic oil were gradually lifted. The powers of the Civil Aeronautics Board (CAB) over the airline industry were reduced, and the agency was eventually abolished. The Reagan administration particularly favored deregulation and the lifting of controls that were deemed obstacles to economic growth.[23]

Our very brief examination of the history of regulation has shown some of the changes in attitudes and practices that have occurred in the last two centuries. From a period of government direction of the economy during the mercantilist era we moved to a time of relative economic freedom as the ideas of classical capitalism prevailed. By the late nineteenth and early twentieth centuries, the growth of trusts and the concentration of economic power led to greater state intervention. The late twentieth century saw another movement to greater economic freedom and deregulation. Whether the pendulum is shifting again in favor of regulation as a result of the failure of thrift institutions and the growth in environmental concerns remains to be seen.

In general, however, the periodic shifts from regulation to greater freedom of action have taken place for at least two reasons. First, economic conditions themselves have changed. Mercantilism developed when strong nation-states under powerful monarchs emerged in Europe and great merchants arose as important political and economic forces.[24] Classical capitalism grew in popularity as manufacturing and industrialization became dominant factors in the economy of Great Britain and, later, in other western nations as well.[25] Regulation grew in favor when giant corporations developed and the perceived threats to competition and popular control of government became common concerns.[26]

A second reason for these shifts is that intellectual or political leaders helped to change people's attitudes concerning how the economy should be run. Adam Smith was the intellectual forefather of modern capitalism. It is harder to point to a single person who developed ideas in support of contemporary policies of regulation, but political leaders such as Theodore Roosevelt and writers such as Herbert Croly and the various muckraking journalists are among those who built support for government controls. The Progressive Era and the New Deal helped to consolidate this trend toward interventionist policies. The Populists and the Progressives made government regulation of economic conditions both palatable and popular, while candidates of the major political parties gradually came to accept the need for public limits on private power.[27]

Issues Concerning Government Regulation

Even as support for government regulation has waxed and waned, certain underlying issues have remained matters of contention. Five of the issues over which proponents and opponents disagree are the appropriate role of government in our society, the best way of achieving happiness and distributing the fruits of an expanding economy, the conditions under which public regulation is appropriate, suitable mechanisms and structures for government intervention, and the effects of regulation on economic competitiveness.

Role of government Supporters of free market economics or traditional capitalism tend to favor a limited role for the state. Government might affect the economy by providing a common currency, protecting private property, enforcing contracts, or helping to build the economic infrastructure (recall Adam Smith's support for the construction and maintenance of public works), but it should do little else. Economic and political freedom are seen as inextricably connected.[28]

Those who favor government regulation of the economy tend to emphasize a more expansive role for the state. They argue that government should protect the common citizen against the predatory behavior of some of the economically powerful. In a modern society, those with wealth and political clout are organized to get what they want, while most people, particularly the poorest and least skilled, must fend for themselves. Those in favor of regulation believe that the government should help to maintain a balance among the various interests of society so that no group becomes overly strong and oppressive. Indeed, government can help to maintain economic freedom by intervening to ensure competition. This justification for antitrust legislation has come to be accepted by many supporters of free enterprise.[29]

Achieving happiness How is happiness to be achieved and the benefits of a modern industrial society to be widely distributed? Adam Smith and his intellectual descendants would probably argue that happiness results from the efforts of free individuals who enter into contractual agreements to work, produce, buy, and sell the services and articles of commerce and industry. Appeals to self-interest are the means of satisfying our wants. As Smith suggests:

> It is not from the benevolence of the butcher, the brewer, or the baker, that we expect our dinner, but from their regard to their own interest. We address ourselves, not to their humanity but to their self-love, and never talk to them of our necessities but of their advantages.[30]

The free market, not government, is the mechanism for distributing economic benefits.

Proponents of government regulation do not deny that individual effort is important in achieving happiness, nor do they argue that self-interest and the free market are irrelevant for satisfying human want. However, they question whether these factors are sufficient to produce equitable treatment of consumers and workers. Without such public measures as the minimum wage, rules to protect the safety of employees in the workplace, and legislation to ensure the purity of food and drugs, they doubt that the majority of people would truly share in the benefits of an advanced economy. Particularly in an age of giant companies and a large, somewhat impersonal society, government regulation is necessary to advance certain social values—justice, safety, and honesty in the marketplace.[31]

When public regulation is appropriate Most people are neither opponents of all public regulation nor advocates of total control of the economic system. The major question that must be resolved is when government restraints are appropriate. Even those who are skeptical about regulatory activities might agree that a case can be made for intervention when there is a natural monopoly or a severe danger to human life or health.

A natural monopoly is created when the technology of an industry or the nature of a service permits the customer to be served at the least cost or greatest benefit only by a single firm or a very limited number of companies. Thus, a public utility is franchised to supply electricity, local telephone service, or gas to customers in a given area because it is unprofitable and impractical for many companies to compete with one another. Under these conditions, there will probably be widespread agreement on controlling prices or profits of the utility.[32]

Those who are more sympathetic to government regulation agree that monopoly conditions and threats to public health are justifications for public restraint on business, but they would add some other conditions as well. Equitable treatment of workers and customers, protection of women and members of minority groups against discrimination, safeguarding of consumers against misleading or incomplete information by business, and the prevention of destructive competition in selected fields have all been used as justifications for regulation.

Some scholars distinguish between economic and social regulation. **Economic regulation** focuses on control over such major economic decisions as price, rate of return, and entry and exit for particular industries. **Social regulation**, on the other hand, tends to concern itself with specific attributes of products affecting several industries, such as matters of safety or health. Social regulation, which has grown since the 1960s, is usually justified by the need to protect the environment, consumers, and workers. Economic regulation has been justified on different grounds: the inability of market conditions to provide adequate control, as in the case of a natural monopoly; the need for a central authority to allocate a common limited resource, such as radio frequencies; the need to provide certain basic services, such as electricity and telephone service, to everyone; the need to prevent cut-throat competitive practices (price discrimination, price wars, and the like) that might drive other companies out of business; the desirability of encouraging the growth of industries during early stages of development, particularly if great risks are involved; and the need to protect existing firms that are part of an already regulated industry.[33]

In general, advocates of reduced regulation wish to allow the private sector to police itself. In the past they tended to shy away from national intervention, favoring state and local control if any had to be imposed. However, the locus of regulation seems to be less important than the extent and stringency of controls in distinguishing between supporters and opponents of more regulation. Some industries, for example, may prefer national safety requirements, because they are uniform and avoid the need for firms to try to comply with a myriad of costly and time-consuming state rules. Similarly, some advocates of greater regulation may wish to allow state and local discretion in establishing standards either because they do not consider national policies to be sufficiently rigorous or because they view national decision-makers as less sympathetic to their concerns.[34]

Mechanisms and structures for government intervention To say that government intervention is necessary or desirable is not to argue that regulation in the conventional sense is the best way to govern the economy. Broadly speaking, there are two means of altering behavior. Direct regulation establishes rules or prohibitions to which people must adhere. Market incentives, on the other hand, provide them with material benefits or costs, depending on the behaviors that they choose. Direct regulation, for example, might require a firm to stop discharging pollutants into a river under pain of criminal prosecution. The same issue could be dealt with by charging a polluter a fee based on the amount of refuse that enters the waterway.[35]

Direct regulation tries to apply rules on a more uniform basis. It relies upon the threat or use of sanctions to produce change. Market incentives give people some choices in determining what they will do. They do not impose very high implementation costs on the government, yet they permit a significant degree of freedom. Unless the incentives to alter behavior are greater than those to continue it, however they may be ineffective.[36]

In the United States the independent agency is one of the most common structures for implementing regulations. The Interstate Commerce Commission was the first independent regulatory body created by federal law. Some other important agencies are the Consumer Product Safety Commission, the Environmental Protection Agency, the Federal Reserve System, the Federal Trade Commission, the National Labor Relations Board, the Nuclear Regulatory Commission, and the Securities and Exchange Commission. Agencies that have regulatory powers may also be designed to aid clientele groups. Thus, the Federal Deposit Insurance Corporation provides insurance on the deposits in most commercial banks, and most of the savings and loan institutions.

Typically, the independent agency with regulatory authority is composed of a commission or collective body appointed by the president for a fixed period of time with the approval of the Senate. Commissioners cannot be removed except for cause (serious misconduct, neglect, or failure to perform one's duties), and they are not directly responsible to the president. Although these agencies are headed by a chairperson who usually has the authority to oversee the staff and set the agenda for meetings, decisions are made collectively. These regulatory bodies are given the power not only to execute policy but also to issue rules having the force of law and to impose penalties for violations. Thus, they are in part quasi-legislative and quasi-judicial agencies. Commissioners or board members usually rely upon the recommendations of staff, including administrative law judges, in rendering decisions.[37]

Critics of the regulatory commissions have argued that too much power has been granted to these bodies without adequate accountability. They are not under direct presidential control, and they are not carefully supervised by Congress. The members are not elected by the voters, nor do the agencies tend to be highly visible.[38]

On the other hand, a study of the Nixon and Ford administrations suggests that presidents can influence the decisions of the commissions through the power of appointment, informal communications, budgeting controls, and the like.[39] It is also true that some of the recently created agencies have been made part of the executive branch (e.g., the National Highway Traffic Safety Administration and the Occupational Safety and Health Administration). Even the head of the Environmental Protection Agency serves at the president's pleasure.

A more basic problem with federal regulators, some people believe, is that they have become too closely enmeshed with the concerns and interests of the very groups they are designed to restrain. Indeed, "capture" theories hold that regulatory agencies are often taken over by the industries whose behavior they are supposed to govern. These theories can be extended to state and local bodies as well.[40] Because regulators usually have broad discretion in making and enforcing rules, this combination of interest-group influence and inadequately checked power weakens the whole system of constitutional accountability.

Not all scholars believe that capture theory adequately describes regulatory policy-making. The notion that agency members are pawns of the regulated interests is not always valid.[41] One could also argue that the independence of many agencies from direct political influence is beneficial. It provides a check on the economic power of the president and Congress and permits some measure of nonpartisan discretion and expertise to come to bear on the decision-making process.

Economic competitiveness There are two aspects of economic competitiveness that can be explored in the effort do determine the effects of government regulation. We can consider the ability of a firm to compete within the complex American economic system and the capability of American business to contend effectively with companies throughout the world.

Advocates of deregulation argue that government rules impose a heavy burden on all businesses, but most particularly on small firms. Compliance with licensing, reporting, and safety requirements, among others, cost owners and managers enormous amounts of time and money. Newly formed enterprises and those with few employees face a dilution of their efforts because they must devote attention to the paperwork that accompanies these regulations.[42]

Some rules designed to help consumers or workers may actually serve to harm them. Critics point to Food and Drug Administration regulations that delay for years the introduction of valuable pharmaceuticals in the United States. The minimum wage, which is meant to help provide workers with a livable income, often acts instead to reduce the employment of younger and less skilled employees while driving up the cost of living.[43]

Internationally, we are competing in an arena in which other nations have become increasingly sophisticated and productive. Some of our most aggressive competitors are in Third World countries, where wages are relatively low. Consequently, they already have an advantage as to the cost of production. Every time we impose additional regulations on American companies, we raise the cost of producing goods in the United States. These added costs are likely to make the existing trade deficit even worse.[44]

How do defenders of regulation answer these criticisms? They respond through a multifaceted approach. First, small businesses are often exempt from the more costly and time-consuming rules. Federal legislation commonly excludes firms employing only a very small number of employees or those having revenues below a certain amount from the full force of national mandates. Second, regulation may actually help businesses that seek to treat workers and consumers fairly by imposing national standards on their competitors and not putting them at a comparative disadvantage. Third, rules are often needed to prevent abuse or injury. Food and Drug Administration requirements may delay the introduction of useful drugs into the United States, but they can also prevent the tragedy of the drug Thalidomide, which caused deformities in many children in the countries where it was distributed. The minimum wage tries to provide workers with a minimally decent standard of living, something which the least skilled and least organized employees might be denied without government assistance. Fourth, deregulation is not without its own dangers, as we have seen with the savings and loan industry. As the rules governing interest rates and investment policies were ended or relaxed, many institutions made questionable loans, and some fell into insolvency as a result of insider abuse or criminal conduct by managers and top executives. Finally, it is difficult to show that regulations automatically lead to greater trade deficits. For example, some of the western countries that have favorable balances of trade place more stringent limits on employers who wish to close plants or lay off workers. These countries compel companies to provide paid vacations of various lengths and some form of leave for new parents. In short, publicly required labor costs have not necessarily prevented successful international competition.[45]

DEREGULATING THE AIRLINE INDUSTRY

The 1970s and 1980s became a period of support for the process of deregulation. The pressure to end restraints and free business from the laws and administrative rules that governed it was probably the result of at least four factors: a belief that existing regulations were often expensive and ineffective; a view that government was frequently intrusive and was the cause of, rather than the solution to, problems; a perception that the American economy was stagnating and had to be energized by a dose of relatively unrestrained competition; and the ascendancy of business-oriented or conservative political leaders in both major parties who articulated the need to reduce economic restraints.[46]

One of the first industries during this time to undergo deregulation was the airlines. Shortly thereafter, the process was repeated with varying degrees of completeness with the railroads, trucking, oil and natural gas industries, banks, and savings and loan institutions. Deregulation of airlines began during the Ford administration, was greatly assisted by the Carter presidency, and was completed during the Reagan years. As we will see, the process involved both executive and legislative initiatives, as well as steps taken by the CAB. It was controversial almost from the very start.

The airline industry had been publicly subsidized since the 1920s, when it began to receive airmail contracts from the federal government. In 1934, as a result of Senate investigations into collusion by large airlines and U.S. Post Office officials in the awarding of contracts, the U.S. Army replaced the airlines as airmail carriers for a short time.

Several army pilots died in a series of accidents because they had little experience and improper equipment. Congress then passed the Airmail Act of 1934, which placed the airline industry under the control of several agencies. The Post Office could determine entry to the industry through the awarding of contracts that determined routes and schedules for airmail. The Interstate Commerce Commission set compensation for mail transport, and the Bureau of Air Commerce was in charge of safety.

In order to fight off competition and to bargain with the government, the major airlines formed the Air Transport Association in 1936. The association sought increased federal aid and protection against "excessive competition." In 1938 Congress passed the Civil Aeronautics Act, which consolidated airline regulation under one agency, a predecessor of the CAB. The CAB controlled most aspects of domestic air transport, with the exception of intrastate carriers, and generally acted to restrict competition in routes and fares.[47]

In the 1960s and 1970s, economists began to question the system of air regulation. Some academic studies suggested that regulated prices were higher than they would be if competitive conditions existed.

After Gerald Ford became president in 1974, he made regulatory reform an important part of his domestic program. The recession, combined with rising prices, led many critics to attack government regulations as anticompetitive, inflationary, and wasteful. Although President Ford asked Congress in the autumn of 1974 to create a commission on regulatory reform to specify areas of needed change, House and Senate panels instead began their own studies of the issue in 1975. In 1975 the president called a "regulatory summit" meeting for key executive branch officials and congressional leaders to discuss reform. He also ordered all executive departments and agencies to "make major improvements in the quality of service" to consumers and to begin an assessment of the "inflationary impact of significant legislation, rules and regulations."

The administration's major legislative proposal in the area of regulating reform was a package of three bills designed to reduce federal controls and increase competition in the transportation industry. Except for limited loosening of controls on railroads in 1976, Congress took no final action on the parts dealing with airlines or trucking. However, House and Senate committees did hold extensive hearings on airline deregulation.[48]

President Ford had many advocates of deregulation in his administration. They were found in the Council on Wage and Price Stability, the Office of Management and Budget, the Department of Transportation, the Council of Economic Advisers, and the Antitrust Division of the Justice Department.

Unfortunately, the chairman of the CAB resisted Ford's anti-inflation and deregulation program. Robert Timm supported rate hikes and endorsed CAB restraints on airline competition. On December 10, 1974, Ford removed Timm from the chairmanship and temporarily appointed another board member, Richard O'Melia, to replace him. A new chairman, John Robson, assumed his position in June 1975. The CAB began to support the move toward deregulation and greater competition after Timm was removed.[49]

The importance of the CAB shift in policy should not be underestimated. Particularly after John Robson resigned the chairmanship, and President Jimmy Carter appointed Alfred Kahn to the post, there was a movement away from restrictions on carrier pricing policies and the encouragement of price competition. Kahn, an economist, led an agency that now actively promoted low-cost air service and competition between charter and scheduled airline travel. The board adopted a recommendation of a study by Roy Pulsifer, a CAB staff member, who urged that fare levels be used as a major criterion in route decisions. Preferential treatment was given to carriers that proposed to introduce low fares on a route. In most cases, carrier price reductions as much as 50 percent below the standard industry rate were approved automatically.[50]

Kahn not only publicly supported deregulation, but he used his power to appoint like-minded individuals to strategic staff positions in the CAB. A reorganization of the CAB staff was carried out by his special assistant, Dennis A. Rapp, who later became managing director of the agency. Persons with pro-deregulation views were appointed as director of a newly created Office of Economic Analysis, head of a new Bureau of Pricing and Domestic Aviation, director of the Bureau of Consumer Protection, and legal counsel.[51]

Kahn had the full support of President Carter. Carter, who had been a small businessman, supported the thrust of regulatory reduction and simplification. The administration favored deregulation of transportation and depository institutions, improved regulatory management (efforts to improve procedures, increase public participation, expand analytical capabilities of agencies, and strengthen presidential control and coordination of regulatory bodies), and regulatory procedural reform legislation (efforts to make rules more cost-effective, providing for review of old rules, and so on).[52]

The airlines providing all-cargo service were the first to undergo deregulation. In November 1977 the president signed into law a statute that entitled airlines already carrying cargo exclusively to all-cargo certificates, giving them authority to operate throughout the country. Most of the CAB's authority to control rates and routes of all-cargo carriers was abolished. Within a year following the law's enactment, other carriers were allowed to apply for all-cargo certificates, which the CAB would be required to grant if they were deemed "fit, willing, and able."[53]

In October 1978 Congress passed legislation that was designed to complete the process of airline deregulation. The law provided for the abolition of the CAB by 1985 unless Congress acted to extend it. It would gradually increase competition in the passenger airline industry, phasing out federal controls over the next seven years. The CAB was instructed to stress competition in its decisions and to expedite and simplify agency procedures. The bill was supportive of airline companies that offered new services and routes, and it allowed them some flexibility in raising and lowering their fares.

Small communities were guaranteed that existing levels of air service would be continued for ten years. Airline employees became eligible for compensation if they lost their jobs, suffered wage cuts, or were forced to relocate as a result of increased industry competition brought about by deregulation.[54]

How did deregulation legislation secure congressional approval? The process was complex, involving a number of actors, but it is clear that there was a bipartisan coalition that transcended the usual ideological divisions.

The push for deregulation, which began in earnest in 1975, made use of several strategies, according to a leading academic study by Anthony Brown. It involved

1. **The articulation of a policy alternative** The policy was phrased in terms of competition rather than regulation.
2. **Policy evaluation** Eight sets of hearings were held by five separate congressional committees, and many reports and studies were conducted by the CAB, the Department of Transportation, the General Accounting Office, and committees of Congress.
3. **Political packaging** The case for deregulation was presented in terms of lower prices and the fight against inflation as well as in terms of equity (e.g., concern for small communities and the employees of airlines).
4. **Strategic compromise** Deregulation was phased in rather than put in force immediately; protections in the 1978 bill were included for small towns and airline workers who might be adversely affected; and benefits were included to allow commuter airlines to carry more passengers in their planes and receive government loans and subsidies, and to permit liberalized rules for charter carriers so that they could attract additional customers.
5. **Strategic staffing** Presidents Ford and Carter used their power of appointment to put people who favored deregulation on the CAB. As noted previously, Chairman Alfred Kahn also filled important posts in his agency with appointees who favored competition and lower prices.
6. **Administrative deregulation** CAB moves to deregulate led to fears that statutory change was needed in order to maintain legislative control of the process. Because it was likely that CAB changes would be challenged in the

courts, legislation would also help to protect policies already in place from being overturned.[55]

The proposed legislation itself went through a metamorphosis. Originally, President Ford called for decremental reform of regulation, which would relax rules concerning rates and entry of new carriers into the transportation industry. On April 28, 1975, in a speech before the national meeting of the Chamber of Commerce, he said that he would submit to Congress "a comprehensive transportation program designed to achieve maximum reform of federal regulations governing our railroad, airline, and trucking firms." In the next few months Ford transmitted bills to relax regulation of railroads and airlines. The Railroad Revitalization and Regulatory Reform Act was passed in 1976. The Aviation Reform Act of 1975 did not meet with such a quick or favorable response.[56]

Senator Edward Kennedy (Democrat, Massachusetts) scheduled hearings on CAB regulation before his Subcommittee on Administrative Practices and Procedure early in 1975. Kennedy's aide, Stephen Breyer, made sure that critics of regulation were given an opportunity to present their case first, and he also ensured that testimony by various agencies would be prepared and delivered by advocates of deregulation.

The Kennedy hearings revealed much dissatisfaction with CAB regulations. Regulated carriers generally supported an incremental approach to reform. They tended to blame specific agency decisions, rather than the structure itself, for any problems that existed. Objections to deregulation were also voiced by those who argued that small communities would be denied service if rate and route competition were encouraged.

Although deregulation supporters did not fully advance arguments to remove these concerns, a study commissioned by the subcommittee refuted a contention of the Air Transport Association that deregulation would result in substantial service reduction. Witnesses also pointed out that predatory pricing and monopolization, which some said would result from deregulation, were already illegal under antitrust laws.[57]

The next major round of hearings occurred before the Senate Commerce Subcommittee on Aviation, chaired by Howard Cannon (Democrat, Nevada). Cannon had originally been a supporter of regulation. The Ford administration sought to convince him of the need to support regulatory reform.

Shortly after the president transmitted the Aviation Reform Act in October 1975, Senator Kennedy introduced similar legislation. The administration measure and the Kennedy bill were considered in the Cannon hearings convened in April 1976.

Neither bill sought total deregulation or the abolition of the CAB. However, both bills included most of the provisions in the final legislation passed by Congress.

Cannon was persuaded to support the administration approach after hearing the testimony of John Robson, who was then chairman of the CAB. Robson said in behalf of the board that the current regulatory system presented great risks and uncertainties and that what was needed was a system that relied on competition and minimized government interference. Cannon endorsed the board's position shortly after the 1976 hearings, stating his belief in the need for regulatory reform.[58]

When Cannon's subcommittee began hearings again in March 1977, they met to consider two bills. One was jointly sponsored by Senators Cannon and Kennedy, while the other was sponsored by Senators James B. Pearson (Republican, Kansas), ranking minority member on the subcommittee, and Howard Baker (Republican, Tennessee), the Senate minority leader.

The Pearson-Baker bill, endorsed by the CAB, would give more discretion to that agency in implementing reforms. Originally introduced after the Ford and Kennedy bills, it was later reintroduced as the Commercial Aviation Regulatory Reform Act of 1977. The Cannon-Kennedy bill was a compromised version of the original Ford and Kennedy bills but included a provision for airline employee compensation, which was designed to weaken labor opposition to reform.

The Senate Commerce Committee reported the Cannon-Kennedy bill, the Air Transportation Regulatory Reform Act of 1978, to the floor of the Senate after lengthy deliberations. During the markup (the period in which the specific provisions of the bill were drafted) the White House lobbied committee members to provide a favorable report. The president had endorsed the Cannon-Kennedy bill when he took office, and the administration now organized interest group support for the measure. The act was passed by the Senate overwhelmingly on April 19, 1978.[59]

In the House, the Public Works Subcommittee on Aviation, chaired by Glenn Anderson (Democrat, California) did not begin markup on a companion bill until March 1978. The most controversial issue to arise was the question of relaxed route regulation.

Elliott Levitas (Democrat, Georgia) secured the approval of an amendment that struck the provisions allowing airlines the right of automatic entry into new routes. When another member of the committee, Allen Ertel (Democrat, Pennsylvania) reinstated the provision, Levitas responded by proposing a new bill to be considered for markup. In most respects it was weaker than the Anderson bill. It deleted most provisions relaxing rate and route regulation. However, the Levitas bill did include a provision to terminate the CAB on December 31, 1983, unless it was reauthorized by Congress; its functions would be transferred to other agencies if it was abolished.

At one point the Levitas bill was approved by the subcommittee. Anderson tried to arrive at a compromise during the next seven weeks. The compromise bill approved by the House Public Works and Transportation Committee included weaker restrictions on CAB regulations than those in the Senate bill. Nevertheless, it retained a version of automatic entry as well as the provision to eliminate the CAB by 1982 unless it was reauthorized. The House approved the bill on September 21, 1978, in a vote of 363 to 8.[60]

In order to reconcile the differing House and Senate versions, a conference committee was created that began to meet on October 2, 1978. The two principal parts of the legislation on which compromise was needed were the automatic-entry provision and the termination of CAB regulatory authority. The Senate conferees agreed to a more conservative entry program, whereby carriers could request annual entry into two routes in 1979, 1980, and 1981. In each year, a carrier could protect one of its routes from entry. However, the House members accepted a phased approach by which CAB authority was gradually ended before a decision was reached regarding agency termination.

The House and Senate accepted the conference committee report. President Carter signed the bill on October 14, 1978.[61]

The passage of the deregulation legislation was not easily accomplished. Some powerful interest groups, including the unions representing airline employees and most of the major airlines, opposed deregulation. Senators George McGovern (Democrat, South Dakota) and Barry Goldwater (Republican, Arizona) cosponsored an amendment to weaken the Cannon-Kennedy bill by limiting the automatic-entry provisions.

However, other interest groups supported the measure. Conservative groups—the American Conservative Union and the National Taxpayers Union—and liberal groups—Americans for Democratic Action and Common Cause—all backed the bill. United Airlines broke with the other giants of the industry to support substantial deregulation. By March 1978, United was joined by Western and Braniff in supporting decontrol.[62]

It is doubtful, however, that deregulation would have come to fruition at that time if there had not been strong initiative from two different presidents—Ford and Carter. It is also true that the actions and testimony of the CAB chairmen, John Robson and Alfred Kahn, probably helped secure the necessary votes for deregulation. Thus, an industry that had been highly regulated for 40 years was made subject to a new and different set of legislative rules.

In the years of the Reagan administration, the process of deregulation was completed. The CAB was allowed to die in 1985, as the 1978 legislation provided. A year before termination of the agency, Congress passed a law to transfer consumer protection powers of the CAB to the Department of Transportation. Thus, the department could consider such matters as controlling smoking on flights, bumping passengers to other flights, and protecting luggage from damage. The Department of Transportation was also given the power to approve antitrust matters such as airline mergers and antitrust exemptions for airlines.[63]

How has deregulation affected the airlines and the people they serve? The answer is somewhat mixed.

On the whole, air fares have risen less rapidly since deregulation than before. Indeed, on a cost-per-mile basis, taking into account price changes since 1978, domestic air fares declined more in the eight years after deregulation than in the eight previous years. However, most savings have occurred because discount fares are increasingly available to people who can make reservations several weeks in advance. Fares for business travelers and those unable to make advance reservations have risen substantially.[64]

Initially, competition among airlines increased as new firms were started or carriers entered routes they had not previously flown. In the early 1980s, however, such companies as Continental and Braniff had to declare bankruptcy. Many of the new carriers were unable to stay in business as independent entities. More recently, there have been mergers and takeovers by Texas Air, US Air, American, and Northwest. There is fear that these consolidations of major airlines will lead to more rapid fare increases and less competition in the years ahead.[65]

Small towns have lost subsidized jet service since deregulation. In many cases, commuter airlines moved in to fill the gap and now provide some flights for these communities.[66]

Since the passage of the 1978 law, airline safety has been an issue, although it was never the subject of deregulation. The Federal Aviation Administration continued to enforce standards with which the airlines were expected to comply. Nevertheless, fear has been expressed that increased competition causes airlines to cut corners on maintenance and inspections so that they can retain their profit margins. This fear may have grown because the Reagan administration in its first term cut the number of Federal Aviation Administration inspectors. Moreover, the average age of planes in service is increasing.

Despite criticism of "near-misses" and poor maintenance practices, safety probably improved in the last decade. On the average, there have been fewer fatalities per year since 1978 and not as many near-misses as in the 1960s.[67]

Although the overall safety record is generally good, some have questioned its quality among the growing number of commuter airlines. The rate of fatalities per million passenger miles is several times greater for commuter carriers than for the major airlines. It has been suggested that this is caused in part by the use of small passenger planes and by the large numbers of less experienced firms that must compete aggressively with one another.[68]

In recent years many customers have complained about flight delays, lost or damaged luggage, and declining service. Efforts have been made to pressure airlines to reduce delays and handle baggage more carefully. The Department of Transportation publishes information available to the public on domestic airlines' records in keeping to their schedules and handling luggage.

Some of the problems with flight delays are only indirectly related to deregulation. The strike of air traffic controllers in 1981 led to the firing of many experienced employees and caused long-term disruption of the traffic-control system in many cities. The absence of new airport construction has also contributed to congestion. Undoubtedly, the need for additional flights to service a growing number of air travelers has compounded the problem.[69]

There may be less service in the form of complete meals, attention to first class customers, and compensation for passengers stranded as a result of cancelled flights. On the other hand, deregulation made it possible for many more Americans to take advantage of low fares and thus become part of the flying public.[70]

Some observers question whether airline employees have benefited from deregulation. Their productivity has risen, but their compensation has declined in relative and sometimes absolute terms. The rash of mergers, bankruptcies, and failed firms caused the dismissal of employees of some major carriers and concessions by the unions that represent airline workers. The 1978 act has not been very effective in helping airline employees who lost jobs because they have the burden of proof in demonstrating that unemployment resulted from deregulation.[71]

SUMMARY

The regulatory policies of American government have changed in response to alterations in economic thought and the conditions of the economy. From the period of mercantilism to that of deregulation, we noted shifts in the extent and nature of public intervention.

The regulation–deregulation controversy, which has been of such great importance in recent years, involves a number of other subsidiary issues. Advocates of each position disagree about such questions as the role of government, the best way of achieving happiness and distributing the fruits of our economy, the conditions under which public regulation is appropriate, suitable mechanisms and structures for government intervention, and the effects of regulation on economic competitiveness.

We briefly examined the successful effort to deregulate domestic airline fares and routes. The legislative struggle to achieve this goal was accomplished through the actions of two presidents, the chairmen of the CAB, important members of Congress, and a coalition of interest groups that was not limited to one ideological orientation.

Deregulation of the airlines has had mixed results. Preliminary evidence suggests that it encouraged competition and produced lower overall fares during most of the post-1978 period than would have occurred if statutory change had not taken place. On the other hand, business travelers have seen a significant increase in air costs and there has been concern about the growing numbers of mergers and takeovers in recent years. Safety does not appear to have been adversely affected, but there is a disparity in the record of major carriers and commuter lines. Some loss of service has occurred in small communities, and there probably has been a loss of amenities in order to permit airlines to offer cut-rate fares and still make a profit. Airline employees, particularly those working for the larger carriers, are generally not doing as well since the Airline Deregulation Act of 1978 was passed.

Government intervention can occur in more than one way. We previously distinguished between two means of altering behavior: direct regulation and the use of market incentives. Somewhat related to the use of market factors is the provision of assistance to workers and producers. The next chapter considers government subsidies and some of their potential effects on the American economy.

NOTES

[1]Excerpt from *An Inquiry Into the Nature and Causes of The Wealth of Nations* in *Adam Smith Today*, ed. Arthur Hugh Jenkins (New York: Richard R. Smith, 1948), p. 456.

[2]"State of the Union Message of 1905," cited in David M. Chalmers, *Neither Socialism nor Monopoly: Theodore Roosevelt and the Decision to Regulate the Railroads* (Philadelphia: Lippincott, 1976), p. 89.

[3]Adam Smith, *An Inquiry Into the Nature and Causes ofThe Wealth ofNations* (New York: Random House, 1937); and Robert L. Heilbroner, *The Worldly Philosophers: The Lives, Times, and Ideas of the Great Economic Thinkers* (6th ed.; New York: Simon & Schuster, 1986), pp. 42–74.

[4]Norman Ware, *Wealth and Welfare: The Backgrounds of American Economics* (New York: William Sloane Associates, 1949), pp. 52–54.

[5]Gary M. Walton, "The Colonial Economy," in Glenn Porter, ed., *Encyclopedia of American Economic History: Studies of the Principal Movements and Ideas*, vol. 1 (New York: Scribner's, 1980), pp. 34–50. Also see Edwin J. Perkins, *The Economy of Colonial America* (New York: Columbia University Press, 1980), particularly Chapters 2 and 7. Perkins argues that the restrictive Navigation Acts did not greatly harm the colonists.

[6]James F. Shepherd, "Economy from the Revolution to 1815," in *Encyclopedia of American Economic History*, vol. 1, pp. 51–65; and Robert L. Heilbroner, with Aaron Singer, *The Economic Transformation of America* (New York: Harcourt Brace Jovanovich, 1977), p. 24.

[7]Shepherd, pp. 51–65; and Ernest L. Bogart and Donald L. Kemmerer, *Economic History of the American People* (New York: Longmans, Green, 1947), pp. 236, 270, 359–360. Clay supported a system of protective tariffs as well as federally supported internal improvements, such as roads and canals.

[8]Bogart and Kemmerer, pp. 532–534.

[9]*Ibid.*, p. 548; James E. Anderson, *The Emergence of the Modern Regulatory State* (Washington, DC: Public Affairs Press, 1962), pp. 92–104; and Gabriel Kolko, *Railroads and Regulation 1877–1916* (Princeton, NJ: Princeton University Press, 1965), pp. 15–16, 34–41. Kolko suggests that railroad interests favored federal regulation partly because they hoped to forestall more radical demands and because they wanted to secure order in an anarchic industry.

[10]Bogart and Kemmerer, p. 502.

[11]*Ibid.*, p. 549.

[12]*Ibid.*

[13]*Ibid.*, p. 504

[14]*Ibid.*

[15]*Ibid.*, pp. 652–654; and Heilbroner and Singer, pp. 194–195.

[16]Bogart and Kemmerer, p. 673.

[17]Ibid., p.621; Heilbroner and Singer, p. 195; and Lloyd D. Musolf, *Promoting the General Welfare: Government and the Economy* (Glenview, IL: Scott, Foresman, 1965), pp. 76–77.

[18]Frederic S. Mishkin, *The Economics of Money, Banking, and Financial Markets* (2d ed.; Glenview, IL: Scott, Foresman, 1989), pp. 63, 223, 227, 340.

[19]Mary A. Yeager, "Bureaucracy," in *Encyclopedia of American Economic History*, vol. 3, pp. 911–914.

[20]Heilbroner and Singer, p. 216; Arthur M. Johnson, "Economy Since 1914," in *Encyclopedia of American Economic History*, vol. 1, p. 120; and Byrd L. Jones, "Government Management of the Economy," in *Encyclopedia of American Economic History*, vol. 2, pp. 820–821.

[21]Johnson, p. 121; and Melvyn Dubofsky, "Labor Organizations," in *Encyclopedia of American Economic History*, vol. 2, p. 542.

[22]Thomas K. McCraw, "Regulatory Agencies," in *Encyclopedia of American Economic History*, vol. 3, pp. 803–804; and Thomas C. Cochran, *Two Hundred Years of American Business* (New York: Basic Books, 1977), p. 248.

[23]Herbert Stein, *Presidential Economics: The Making of Economic Policy from Roosevelt to Reagan and Beyond* (New York: Simon & Schuster, 1984), pp. 20–21, 265, 309; and Larry N. Gerston, Cynthia Fraleigh, and Robert Schwab, *The Deregulated Society* (Pacific Grove, CA: Brooks/Cole, 1988), pp. 41–63.

[24]Ware, pp. 53, 57.

[25]*Ibid.*, pp. 102–119, 128.

[26]Bogart and Kemmerer, pp. 488–506.

[27]Richard Hofstadter, *The Age of Reform: From Bryan to F.D.R.* (New York: Knopf, 1955).

[28]See W. Allen Wallis, *An Overgoverned Society* (New York: Free Press, 1976); Milton Friedman, with Rose D. Friedman, *Capitalism and Freedom* (Chicago: University of Chicago Press, 1962); and Ayn Rand, *Capitalism: The Unknown Ideal* (New York: New American Library, 1966).

[29]Anderson, pp. 76–78, 126–137.

[30]Smith, p. 14.

[31]Gerston, Fraleigh, and Schwab, pp. 22–34.

[32]For a discussion of natural monopoly, see Alfred E. Kahn, *The Economics of Regulation: Principles and Institutions*, vol. 2 (Cambridge, MA: MIT Press, 1988), pp. 2, 113–171.

[33]Gerston, Fraleigh, and Schwab, pp. 24–27.

[34]Although insurance companies have generally preferred state rather than national regulation, there has been resistance on the part of industry to complying with state or local restrictions dealing with auto emissions, labeling of toxic substances, and so on. The preference is generally for national regulation. Also see fn 9.

[35]For a discussion of these contrasting approaches to making public policy, see Charles L. Schultze, *Public Use of Private Interest* (Washington, DC: Brookings Institution, 1977).

[36]For a consideration of some of the problems associated with employing market incentives, see Schultze, pp. 28–43.

[37]For a description of the operation of federal regulatory agencies, see Louis M. Kohlmeier, Jr., *The Regulators: Watchdog Agencies and the Public Interest* (New York: Harper & Row, Pub. 1969).

[38]*Ibid.*, pp. 17–26; and Theodore Lowi, *The End of Liberalism* (New York: W. W. Norton & Co., Inc., 1969), pp. 132–145.

[39]William E. Brigman, "The Executive Branch and the Independent Regulatory Agencies," *Presidential Studies Quarterly*, 11 (Spring 1981), 244–261.

[40]For a brief discussion of capture theories, see Martha Derthick and Paul J. Quirk, *The Politics of Deregulation* (Washington, DC: Brookings Institution, 1985), pp. 91–93. Also see Paul J. Quirk, *Industry Influence in Federal Regulatory Agencies* (Princeton, NJ: Princeton University Press, 1981).

[41]See, for example, Roger G. Noll and Bruce M. Owen, *The Political Economy of Deregulation: Interest Groups in the Regulatory Process* (Washington DC: American Enterprise Institute for Public Policy Research, 1983), pp. 155–162.

[42]William E. Simon, *A Time for Truth* (New York: McGraw-Hill, 1978), pp. 92–93, 102–103.

[43]Noll and Owen, pp. 13–16; and " Minimum Wage Controversy," *Congressional Digest*, 68 (May 1989), 131, 135, 160.

[44]Usually, the argument is made of an indirect nexus between regulation and a decline in our ability to compete internationally. It is suggested that regulation siphons needed money for investment and thus lowers productivity. See, for example, William E. Simon, *A Time for Action* (New York: Reader's Digest Press, 1980), pp. 5, 101.

[45] "Savings and Loan Controversy," *Congressional Digest*, 68 (June–July 1989), 166–167, 192; Frederick C. Thayer, *Rebuilding America: The Case for Economic Regulation* (New York: Praeger, 1984); Robert Lekachman, *Greed Is Not Enough* (New York: Pantheon, 1982), pp. 103–119; "Minimum Wage Controversy," 139ff.; Milton Silverman and Philip R. Lee, *Pills, Profits, and Politics* (Los Angeles: University of California Press, 1974), pp. 94–97; and Lester C. Thurow, *The Zero-Sum Society: Distribution and The Possibilities for Economic Change* (New York: Penguin, 1981), pp. 139–140.

[46]For a discussion of the movement toward deregulation, see Gerston, Fraleigh, and Schwab, pp. 13–16, 34–36, and 40–61.

[47]*Ibid.*, pp. 86–88.

[48]*Ibid.*, p. 89; and *Congress and the Nation: 1973–1976* (Washington, DC: Congressional Quarterly, 1977), pp. 444, 546–547, and 554.

[49]Anthony E. Brown, *The Politics of Airline Deregulation* (Knoxville: University of Tennessee Press, 1987), pp. 106–112, 152.

[50]*Ibid.*, pp. 112, 117.

[51]*Ibid.*, pp. 153–154.

[52]James E. Anderson, "The Carter Administration and Regulatory Reform: Searching for the Right Way," p. 3. Paper presented at the Annual Meeting of the Midwest Political Science Association, Chicago, IL, April 13–15, 1989.

[53]*Congress and the Nation: 1977-1980* (Washington, D.C.: Congressional Quarterly, Inc., 1981), p. 299.

[54]*Ibid.*, p. 311.

[55]Brown, pp. 129–158.

[56]*Ibid.*, pp. 110–111.

[57]*Ibid.*, pp. 107–109.

[58]*Ibid.*, pp. 110–114.

[59]*Ibid.*, pp. 114–115.

[60]*Ibid.*, pp. 119–120.

[61]*Ibid.*, pp. 121–122.

[62]*Ibid.*, p. 118; and Gerston, Fraleigh, and Schwab, pp. 90–91.

[63]*Congress and the Nation: 1981–1984* (Washington, DC: Congressional Quarterly, 1985), pp. 325–326.

[64]Gerston, Fraleigh, and Schwab, pp. 100–102; U.S. Congress, Congressional Budget Office, *Policies for the Deregulated Airline Industry* (Washington, DC: Brooks/Cole 1988), pp. 4–6; and Hal Gieseking, "Flying the Friendly Skies a Decade After Deregulation," *Travel-Holiday* (November 1988), 79.

[65]Gerston, Freleigh, and Schwab, p. 102; and *Policies for the Deregulated Airline Industry*, pp. 11–16.

[66]Gerston, Fraleigh, and Schwab, pp. 103–104.

[67]Gieseking, 79–81; *Policies for the Deregulated Airlines Industry*, pp. 16–18; and Gerston, Fraleigh, and Schwab, pp. 104–106.

[68]Ed Sussman, "'Hey Lou, This Propeller Looks Pretty Sturdy to Me,'" *The Washington Monthly* (November 1988), 32–37.

[69]Gieseking, p. 80.

[70]*Ibid.*, 80–81.

[71]Gerston, Fraleigh, and Schwab, pp. 106–108; and *Policies for the Deregulated Airline Industry*, p. 5.

CHAPTER SEVEN

Economic Subsidies

> Commerce is a perpetual and peaceable war of wit and energy among all nations .... Each nation works incessantly to have its legitimate share of commerce or to gain an advantage over another nation.[1]
>
> *Jean-Baptiste Colbert*

What the seventeenth-century French official Colbert said of the commercial struggle among nations is no less true of the struggle within countries. Today almost every sector of the economy and most of the major actors receive some form of aid from the government. States and localities ply businesses with a wide array of incentives to induce them to settle within their borders or expand their operations. Loans, grants, tax abatements, and the provision of land or buildings at low cost are among the many ways in which economic development is promoted.

The national authorities are no less active in aiding the economy. Federal economic subsidies take a variety of forms, including price supports for agricultural commodities, training programs for unemployed workers, aid to the maritime industry, and tariffs and other restrictions on imported goods. Broadly speaking, subsidies are of two kinds: direct and indirect (Table 7–1). **Direct subsidies** are payments and material benefits given to particular persons or companies to promote or assist certain activities. **Indirect subsidies** include taxes or regulations designed to aid certain actors by reducing competition or giving them an advantage over others. For the purpose of our discussion, the term **subsidies** refers to assistance given to producers or workers to enable them to become more productive, stay in business, or become more competitive.[2]

Subsidies have been with us for hundreds of years. During the mercantilist era of the seventeenth and eighteenth centuries, bounties were given to craftsmen and manufacturers who could help to increase national wealth by exporting their goods abroad. Cabotage laws, which restricted the carrying of merchandise to the

TABLE 7–1 Types of Economic Subsidies

Kinds of Economic Subsidies	Intended Beneficiaries
Direct Subsidies	
Cash payments	Farmers, selected industries
Training and educational grants	Workers and businesses that employ them
Research funds	Businesses, research institutes, colleges and universities, etc.
Loans and loan guarantees	Farmers, selected businesses, students
Indirect Subsidies	
Tax credits and deductions	Selected businesses and occasionally purchasers of certain goods or services
Tariffs	Domestic producers
Regulations (trade quotas, licenses, production limits, minimum wage, etc.)	Existing businesses and some farmers and workers

flag ships of one's own country, were enacted to aid the national merchant marine. In fact, many of the policies of the mercantilist period have persisted in some form to the present day. Although they sometimes met with resistance during the rise of modern capitalism, programs of economic aid continued in advanced industrialized nations and have been common in the less developed countries, where government is often the most prominent economic actor.[3]

Many justifications have been advanced for granting subsidies. Among the most common are compensating for market failure; enhancing national security; assisting new industries; adding to the reserve of human capital; and preventing adverse effects on producers, workers, or consumers.

Market failure occurs when normal controls and mechanisms of the marketplace cannot adequately serve to regulate production, distribution, and pricing of goods or services. One form of market failure exists when there is a natural monopoly, and only one company or a small number of firms can provide a desired service or product at least cost or greatest benefit to consumers. This type of market failure will probably lead to licensing and regulation, as in the case of public utilities. Another type of market failure is exemplified by the collapse of enterprises as a result of outside forces over which the producer has no control (weather conditions, war, upheaval in other countries, and so on). There are those who wish to aid farmers and other entrepreneurs whose failure, they believe, lessens competition and produces great suffering.[4]

Some industries, such as weapons production, mineral extraction, and steel manufacturing, are seen as playing a particularly vital role in the defense of the nation. Subsidies are supported if there is a fear that these industries cannot compete adequately with foreign competitors. Indeed, assistance to our merchant marine has often been justified on that basis.[5]

Protective tariffs are advocated by those who seek to protect new industries that might be vulnerable to foreign competition. As Alexander Hamilton suggested in "The Report on the Subject of Manufacturers" (1791):

> ... the greatest obstacle of all to the successful prosecution of a new branch of industry in a country, in which it was before unknown, consists, as far as the instances apply, in the bounties, premiums and other aids which are granted, in a variety of cases, by the nations, in which the establishments to be initiated are previously introduced. It is well known...that certain nations grant bounties on the exportation of particular commodities, to enable their own workmen to undersell and supplant all competitors, in the countries to which those commodities are sent.[6]

Hamilton recognized the difficulties that new industries so often encounter in attempting to compete with publicly financed firms in other nations.

Economists have long noted that wealth is produced not only by the use of plant and machinery, but by the application and efforts of workers. If the skills of workers increase, then one can expect, other things being equal, that production will grow. Thus, investment in education and training programs to help workers become more skilled—human capital development—is supported as a means of improving productivity.[7]

Sometimes subsidies are provided to certain economic actors in order to prevent suffering. For example, aid to Chrysler was justified when the company was on the verge of bankruptcy on the grounds that its closure would create large-scale unemployment and damage to many communities. In a more subtle way, loans and grants to promote economic development are defended as a means of providing additional jobs and protecting the tax base of a community or state, thus preventing it from being overwhelmed by adverse economic conditions.[8]

Opponents of subsidies also occasionally raise equity arguments.[9] How do we justify helping one company and not another? Why is one industry "bailed out" by the federal government, while others must struggle to survive without direct aid? Is it just to give a high proportion of farm price-support payments to large landowners? It sometimes seems to casual observers as if those interests with money, contacts, and well-organized political action committees can get what they want, regardless of their need or the merits of their proposals.[10]

TWO APPROACHES TO HELPING AMERICAN BUSINESS

It is difficult to understand government assistance programs for the private sector because there are many types of aid provided and the approaches to subsidies are not consistent. In some cases aid is given, while in others it is denied. We can better understand the dynamics of the decision-making process by examining two different ways in which the executive and legislative branches fashioned policies to help American business. The first, the plan to aid Chrysler, illustrates an interventionist approach to save a major firm from financial collapse. The second, the free-trade agreement with Canada, suggests a more subtle means of assisting our producers by opening up additional markets.

The Chrysler Loan Guarantee

By 1979, the Chrysler Corporation was in serious financial difficulty. In the third quarter of 1978, Chrysler lost a record $158.8 million. When Lee Iacocca became president in November 1978, he found a company in disarray. Its British subsidiary was suffering heavy losses. Management was not organized effectively to ensure that experienced specialists would head major corporate divisions. Financial controls to help people in operations save money and make a profit were lacking. Quality control in manufacturing was in dire need of improvement. The company faced major competitive pressure not only from General Motors and Ford, but from the growing threat of Japanese auto makers as well.[11]

The national and international environments were inhospitable for all of the domestic automobile manufacturers. As 1979 began, the pro-American government of Iran fell, and the new regime started to goad the Organization of Petroleum Exporting Countries (OPEC) to raise prices of crude oil. Disruptions of oil supplies and reductions in U.S. reserves created a significant shortage of gasoline. In April, President Carter proposed a new energy policy that called for gradual decontrol of oil prices. The combination of gasoline shortages and rising prices sharply curtailed demand from prospective automobile purchasers.[12]

By the end of 1979, Chrysler was rapidly losing money and looking forward to massive deficits. Indeed, it appeared as if the company would be forced into bankruptcy.

John Riccardo, Chairman of the Board of Directors at Chrysler, first approached the White House about possible aid in December 1978. Speaking to Stuart Eizenstat, the president's chief domestic policy adviser, he blamed the government for many of the financial strains that the company was undergoing. He said that half the retooling scheduled for the next five years was due to government regulations. Chrysler needed a two-year delay in having to comply with certain federal rules. Riccardo emphasized that he did not want a loan similar to that given to the Lockheed Aircraft Corporation. Lockheed had received $250 million in bank loans that were guaranteed by the federal government. Riccardo feared that such an arrangement would ultimately undercut sales and hurt Chrysler more than it helped as a result of unfavorable publicity.[13]

As the financial health of the company deteriorated and sales and revenues continued to decline, it became clear that further action was necessary. On August 9, 1979, Chrysler officials made their first formal plea for federal assistance.[14]

The initial request for a $1 billion advance was rejected by the administration, but Secretary of the Treasury G. William Miller said that the government would consider loan guarantees to help secure private funds. When the company proposed $1.2 billion in loan guarantees on September 15, Miller rejected it as "way out of line." The administration reconsidered the request and agreed to sponsor necessary legislation on November 1, 1979, after Chrysler reported a third-quarter loss of $460 million.[15]

Secretary Miller stated at a news conference that the administration was raising its original plans for a $750 million loan guarantee to $1.5 billion. Based on studies by the Treasury Department, it appeared that the company might need up to $3 billion in the next few years if it was to return to profitability. Miller warned of dire economic consequences for communities around the country if Chrysler were permitted to fail.[16]

Miller told House and Senate leaders that loan guarantees were contingent on the company's raising another $1.5 billion. It would have to sell assets and secure pledges of aid from creditors, workers, and localities in order to do so. Although the administration had wanted to have these commitments when it recommended its bill, it decided to proceed without them because the financial condition of the company was rapidly deteriorating.[17]

Shortly after administration's support was announced, the banking committees of the House and Senate wrote separate bills granting loan guarantees to Chrysler. The House bill was closer to the administration proposal, authorizing $1.5 billion in guarantees and requiring the company to raise a matching sum. It also required Chrysler to issue 10 million new shares of stock for an employee stock ownership plan.[18]

The Senate committee wanted Chrysler workers to make additional sacrifices. It adopted a plan similar to one proposed by Paul E. Tsongas (Democrat, Massachusetts) and Richard G. Lugar (Republican, Indiana), which mandated $1.25 billion in company savings from a three-year wage freeze for union and nonunion employees and $1.43 billion in contributions from other sources.[19]

Opposition to the House and Senate measures came from various sources. Some members, such as Congressmen Richard Kelly (Republican, Florida) and Ron Paul (Republican, Texas), were opposed to help for Chrysler partly on ideological grounds. They did not believe that the government should intervene to save a company that was failing. Other opponents contended it would set a bad precedent and cause more firms to request federal assistance in the years ahead. United Auto Workers (UAW) President Douglas A. Fraser said that his union would oppose reopening a recently negotiated contract because the workers had already agreed to $203 million in savings.[20]

The House and Senate committees delayed reporting their measures to the floor until December 6. In response to the Senate committee's requirement for a three-year wage freeze, the House Banking Committee revised its bill to raise UAW concessions to $400 million. It also increased the employee stock option contribution to $150 million.[21]

The House approved the revised committee measure by a vote of 271 to 136; 62 Republicans and 209 Democrats supported the bill, while 88 Republicans and 48 Democrats opposed it. The victory was the result of skilled lobbying by the administration, the Democratic leadership of the House, the UAW, Chrysler, small businessowners whose interests would be adversely affected by the corporation's failure, and major associations of state and local chief executives. It also came about because there was no organized opposition.[22]

On December 19, three senators from states with large Chrysler facilities—Thomas F. Eagleton (Democrat, Missouri), Joseph R. Biden, Jr. (Democrat, Delaware), and William V. Roth Jr., (Republican, Delaware)—proposed a $3.2 billion substitute for the Senate committee's plan. It would reduce union pay concessions to $400 million. Despite opposition from Senator Lugar, the Senate approved the substitute bill by 54 to 43, but several senators forced its sponsors to withdraw it by threatening a filibuster.[23]

Negotiations were held in the office of Majority Leader Robert C. Byrd (Democrat, West Virginia), with Banking Committee leaders and Chrysler proponents. A $3.6 billion compromise was hammered out to provide federal loan guarantees of $1.5 billion and union concessions of $525 million. The Senate approved the compromise by a 69 to 28 vote and then passed the amended measure late in the day.[24]

In order to reconcile the different versions of the House and Senate measures, a conference committee was formed. For the most part conferees split the difference on provisions that were in conflict after a long meeting on December 20, at which Chrysler officials and UAW leaders were present. The conference committee agreed to a $3.5 billion package, which included $1.5 billion in loan guarantees, $462.5 million in UAW wage concessions over three years, and $125 million in concessions by management employees.[25]

The House passed the conference committee proposal late that evening by a vote of 241 to 124. Despite a short filibuster by William L. Armstrong (Republican, Colorado), who complained that there was inadequate time to study its provisions, the Senate approved the legislation early on the morning of December 21 by a vote of 43 to 34.[26]

The following are the most important provisions of the Chrysler Corporation Loan Guarantee Act:[27]

1. Authorized $1.5 billion in federal loan guarantees.
2. Established a loan guarantee board, consisting of the secretary of the Treasury, comptroller general, and chairman of the Federal Reserve Board, with the secretaries of labor and transportation as nonvoting members. The loan guarantee board would actually make the guarantees.
3. Limited the board's authority to make guarantees to no later than December 31, 1983, and provided that loans that were guaranteed had to be repaid by December 31, 1990.
4. Required that Chrysler secure $1,430,000,000 in additional assistance before the board made loan guarantees. This money would include at least $500,000,000 from domestic lenders, of which $100,000,000 should be concessions on existing debt; at least $150,000,000 from foreign sources; at

least $300,000,000 from the sale of corporate assets; at least $250,000,000 from state and local governments; at least $180,000,000 from suppliers and dealers; and at least $50,000,000 from the sale of additional stock. The loan guarantee board could modify the plan, as long as private contributions amounted to $1,430,000,000.

5. Required unionized workers to accept $462,500,000 in wage reductions under their 1979–1982 contract, including $203,000,000 already agreed to in contract talks.
6. Required at least $125,000,000 in wage concessions by nonunion employees.
7. Mandated Chrysler to issue $162,500,000 in new common stock for a board-approved employee stock ownership plan.

The loan guarantees for Chrysler had to be implemented in part by the Reagan administration. Although Secretary of the Treasury Miller and Fed Chairman Volcker had already begun to wring concessions from domestic banks in the waning days of the Carter presidency, and although many of Chrysler's suppliers had agreed to delayed payments, more remained to be done.[28]

Members of the new administration were not enthusiastic about the loan-guarantee program. Indeed, David Stockman, the new head of the Office of Management and Budget, had been one of the more outspoken critics of the Loan Guarantee Act when he was a congressman from Michigan. While there would be no attempt to dismantle the program, little attention would be given to it at the highest levels of government, and most of the functions of the loan-guarantee board were delegated to career civil servants.[29]

In February 1981, the loan board approved $400 million in additional guarantees. Secretary of the Treasury Donald Regan indicated that the decision to do so had been made by the previous administration, and he said that much more study would have to take place if approval was to be given in the future for the final $300 million in loan-guarantee authority. The loan board did not meet again until the summer of 1983.[30]

It is not difficult to understand why the Reagan administration wanted to distance itself from the loan-guarantee program. The losses suffered by Chrysler were $1.7 billion in 1980, and it seemed to many people that the company might go under in 1981. Despite the reluctance of the administration to help secure additional loan guarantees to aid in the Chrysler bailout, it took two actions that were to be of real assistance to the company. The first involved provisions of the Economic Recovery Tax Act of 1981, which permitted money-losing companies to sell and then promptly lease back plant and equipment to profitable firms, which could receive tax benefits through accelerated depreciation. The Internal Revenue Service (IRS) gave a rapid ruling that permitted the money-losing companies to clear tax-leasing deals in advance with secured creditors, so that the firms that purchased equipment were assured that they could retain tax benefits even if the sellers went into bankruptcy. Shortly thereafter, Chrysler transferred to the General Electric Credit Corporation tax benefits on $100 million worth of Chrysler equipment. From 1981 to 1983, Chrysler received more than $68 million from tax leasing arrangements.[31]

The second and more important benefit was one given not only to Chrysler but to all three major American automakers. Acting in response to pressure from Ford, General Motors, and Chrysler and growing protectionist sentiment in Congress, the White House pressured the Japanese government to limit its growing share of the American auto market.

By early 1981 the Japanese had captured nearly 25 percent of new automobile sales, and Senator John Danforth (Republican, Missouri) had introduced legislation to reduce Japanese imports to 1.6 million cars a year. Officials in Japan were reluctant to impose quotas on its exporters unless the United States government openly demanded that it do so. However, after they saw growing support for the Danforth bill in Congress and were advised by William Brock, the U.S. trade representative, of the political acceptability of various alternative Japanese proposals to restrain exports, they agreed to set limits on the sale of their cars in the United States. On April 30, 1981, Japan's Ministry of International Trade and Industry announced that it would limit exports to the United States to 1.68 million units for the year beginning April 1, 1981. The following year Japanese imports would be limited to 16.5 percent of the total expansion of the market.[32]

In essence, the Japanese auto quotas were an indirect subsidy to the domestic industry, because they allowed it to capture a larger share of the market and raise prices on their cars. Nothing was required from the automakers, their employees, or anyone else dependent on the industry in order to profit from this arrangement.[33]

Although Chrysler's auto production continued to lose money in 1982, the company made a net profit of $170 million as a result of the sale of its tank division, Chrysler Defense. Any profit was notable, because 1982 was the year of the postwar recession, a time when new auto sales plummeted.[34]

By 1983 Chrysler was clearly in a profitable position. By summer it had paid back $1.2 billion in federally guaranteed loans. In fact, by September of that year the federal government even made a profit of $311 million.[35]

In 1980 the Treasury and private banks had received warrants that could be exercised to buy a share of Chrysler common stock for $13 for each warrant surrendered. At the time the warrants were granted, the stock was selling for about $6 per share, but the Treasury had collected 14.4 million of them so that if the rescue succeeded, Chrysler's stockholders would have to share some of their gain. By 1983, Chrysler stock was nearing $30 a share. Initially, Lee Iaccoca wanted the government simply to surrender the securities because the notes that were guaranteed were going to be paid off seven years before they were due and there was no further risk. This request was rejected, and after several months of negotiations, Chrysler and the government still disagreed about the price for the warrants. The Treasury announced its intentions to sell them on the open market to the highest bidder. This meant that warrants could be sold or traded for stock until 1990. If the warrants were exercised, the corporation's stock would be diluted. Chrysler bid to buy the warrants for slightly more than $21 each; it was the highest bidder.[36]

If one considers the plan to assist the Chrysler Corporation based on its outcome, it appears that it succeeded in its primary objective: to save the company from financial failure. Are there, however, other lessons to be drawn from this experience?

Clearly, the passage of the loan-guarantee plan shows the importance of lobbying and group pressure on the legislative process. It is also apparent that the loan-guarantee plan was only one of several steps taken by the federal government that revived Chrysler. It is questionable whether the company would have been restored to profitability so soon had it not been for tax relief and the Japanese agreement to establish quotas on its export of automobiles.

Perhaps the most interesting implication of the Chrysler aid program is that public help served to increase private assistance. As Robert Reich and John Donahue noted:

> Public involvement actually *increased* private commitment to the rescue. This was in large measure because the public money was strictly contingent on private sacrifice....Even those who criticized the system's details or who thought the goal of saving Chrysler was in itself profoundly wrongheaded agreed that the conditionality tactic worked well.[37]

The role of government as intervener and stimulator of private action is one to which we will return in the final chapter.

United States–Canada Free-Trade Agreement

If the Chrysler bailout represents one way in which government can help the private sector, the free-trade agreement with Canada exemplifies a very different approach. This bilateral agreement seeks to open markets and eliminate obstacles to the exchange of goods and services between the two nations. It supports the process of "desubsidization."

Canada and the United States are the two closest trading partners in the world. In 1987, for example, the United States exported $80.3 billion in merchandise and services to Canada and imported $82.9 billion from that country. If present trends continue, the two-way trade will reach $200 billion or more by the early 1990s. During the last several years, Canada has been running a trade surplus with the United States.[38]

Although Canada has profited from the extensive trade with the United States, it has also fallen into a state of dependency. With a population only one-tenth that of its southern neighbor, Canada has not generated enough capital on its own to develop the vast territory under its control. Unlike other technologically advanced western countries, about 40 percent of its economy is foreign-owned. Since the end of World War II, the United States has become the largest investor; today, American firms own over one-fifth of Canada's productive capacity.[39]

If Canadians sometimes felt apprehensive about the growing American influence on their economic and cultural life, businessowners and farmers in the United

States also believed that they were not always able to compete fairly with Canadian producers. Owners of lumber companies complained about the importation of wood products from Canada, claiming that the industry was subsidized by the Canadian governments. American banks were not able to establish a foothold in Canada because of the restrictive regulations of the federal and provincial governments. National and provincial rules governing agriculture made it difficult for farmers to sell milk and poultry products. Even though about 85 percent of the goods between the two nations could already move across the border without the payment of tariffs, trade restrictions continued to place obstacles in the way of free economic relationships.[40]

The Reagan administration favored the establishment of a free-trade agreement and found a willing partner in the Mulroney government in Canada. The Republican platform in 1980 included vague but generally sympathetic language that hinted at an expansion of the economic relationship between the two democracies:

> We will work closely with Canada as our most important trading partner in the hemisphere. We will foster the deep affinity that exists between our two nations and our policies will be based on mutual understanding and complete equality.
> We will seek a North American Accord designed to foster close cooperation and mutual benefit between the United States, Canada, and Mexico.[41]

After Brian Mulroney became prime minister in 1984, with an overwhelming Conservative majority in the Canadian House of Commons, the stage was set to begin serious negotiations on an agreement to facilitate commercial dealings. Unlike the Liberal government that preceded it, the Conservative leadership was generally favorable toward increased American investment and was less inclined to worry about United States economic influence.[42]

The free-trade negotiations between Canada and the United States began in May 1986 and continued through October 1987. The talks started amid growing protectionist sentiment in Congress, and with a realization that in 1992 the members of the European Common Market were scheduled to drop all trade barriers among them and form the most populous international economic union in the world.[43]

When the discussions began, the United States imposed a special duty on shakes and shingles from Canada. In September 1987 it imposed preliminary duties of up to 85 percent on Canadian potash. These actions angered the Canadian prime minister and led him to seek a trade agreement that would protect Canadian interests from arbitrary action by its American trading partner.[44] Many issues were raised as the talks proceeded, of which the following were among the most important:

Subsidies A common American complaint was that Canada subsidized many of its industries, giving them an unfair advantage when they sold their goods in the United States. The Canadians wanted a clear definition of what constituted a subsidy and a list of subsidies that were acceptable and unacceptable. Prime Minister Mulroney called for the creation of a binational panel with the final power to settle trade disputes, including questions about subsidies.

Simon Reisman, the chief Canadian negotiator, insisted that these demands be addressed. The United States responded with a narrow definition of subsidies and classified most federal regional development assistance to the private sector as unfair export support. The Canadians asserted that federal and provincial governments must be permitted to promote economic development in poor regions. The Americans did not produce a proposal for a dispute-settling body. Instead, they presented their own demands for dropping discriminatory provisions in the Canadian tax code that prevented advertising in Canadian editions of American-owned magazines and on U.S. broadcasting stations along the border, and for ending the refund of import duties on cars shipped into Canada if overseas automakers bought Canadian-made parts. Reisman responded to this deadlock at the end of September 1987 by temporarily walking out of the negotiations.[45]

Culture Many Canadians have been concerned about the cultural penetration of their country by the United States. About 90 percent of the Canadian people live within 200 miles of the southern border. They can often receive radio and television broadcasts from the United States. Most of the English-language entertainment programs shown on Canadian television are American-made, as are the films shown in the cinemas. Publishing houses are often subsidiaries of American-controlled firms. Many of the magazines and books sold in Canada are produced in the United States. Canadian nationalists fear that their country runs the risk of losing its distinctive identity, and instead is becoming an American clone.

In order to satisfy domestic concerns, Canadian negotiators sought to remove cultural policy as far as possible from the talks concerning free trade. Nevertheless, tariffs on phonograph records were to be eliminated, thus raising questions about the Canadian recording industry. Moreover, the United States is free to retaliate if it suffers losses as a result of new restrictions on cultural industries.[46]

Energy In the past, Canadian energy policies had sometimes frustrated Americans. The Liberal government of Pierre Trudeau, which was in power for most of the 16 years prior to the accession of Brian Mulroney as prime minister, sought to reduce foreign ownership of resources. It temporarily cut exports of oil to the United States during the Arab oil embargo in the early 1970s and imposed a system of export taxes and export price controls that raised prices to American consumers. Canada limited the export of electricity to the United States and forced Americans to pay higher prices.

The United States in turn controlled natural gas prices at the wellhead, holding them below market levels and thus preventing Canadian exports of this resource. It pursued energy policies designed to increase the use of coal but did not try to resolve the acid-rain problems created by sulphur dioxide emissions. From 1964 to 1975, the United States denied Canadian producers access to its facilities to enrich uranium ore, thus closing its market to this export. It also denied West Coast Canadian refiners the opportunity to buy lower-cost Alaskan crude oil.

The free-trade agreement banned most border restraints and price requirements on the energy trade. It also made it easier for American companies to purchase electricity from Canada. Barriers to the export and enrichment of Canadian uranium were lifted.[47]

Auto Trade Tariff barriers on the two-way automotive trade had largely been eliminated as the result of a 1965 agreement between Canada and the United States. The auto sector makes up about one-third of the bilateral merchandise trade and is its largest component.

The free-trade agreement provided for the elimination of duty remissions, by which firms were induced to produce in Canada. It also mandated an end to the embargo on used cars within five years.[48]

Services The service sector was an area of trade that the United States dominated. Although the United States ran a merchandise trade deficit, it had a substantial surplus in the trade in services. While leaving in place most existing trade restrictions, the free-trade agreement set an obligation on both countries not to introduce new laws and regulations that hinder the exchange of services.

The pact also continues the movement toward deregulation of financial services—commercial banking, investment banking, and trust and loan companies. It seeks to remove most restrictions on the operation and ownership of banks by the nationals of either country. Because Canadian bank regulations have generally had a more restrictive effect on American banks, those firms will be the primary beneficiaries of the changes made.[49]

Investment Although aggregate American investments in Canada are great, per capita Canadian investment in the United States is actually larger. Moreover, Canadian investment in the United States grew at a faster rate from 1982 through 1986 than did American investment in Canada.

Both countries restrict investment by foreign nationals in sensitive industries (e.g., radio stations and shipping in the United States and cultural activities in Canada). Existing restrictions in both countries are "grandfathered," but future policies and regulations must generally be nondiscriminatory. Transportation services, basic telecommunications, and cultural industries are excluded from these provisions.[50]

The many provisions of this complex agreement were hammered out with difficulty. Both sides ultimately accepted a binational panel to arbitrate disputes after all existing measures used by the two countries were exhausted. On October 3, 1987, Canadian and American negotiators announced an agreement in principle, just meeting a deadline established by Congress that would permit a "fast-track" consideration of the agreement without formal amendment by the legislative branch.[51]

President Reagan and Prime Minister Mulroney signed the accord on January 2, 1988. The administration then submitted the agreement to Congress, along with a bill to put it into effect.[52]

The agreement was not a major issue in the United States, but specific provisions soon came under attack. Although its purpose was to eliminate all tariffs between the two countries by 1998, Western senators and textile producers worried about injury to selected sectors of the American economy. Senator Alan K. Simpson (Republican, Wyoming) said that he would vote against the agreement because it endangered petroleum, mineral, and wheat interests vital to his state. Senator Pete V. Domenici (Republican, New Mexico) was concerned that the pact would override a statute that limited uranium imports, thus hurting an industry already reeling as a result of lessened demand from the nuclear-power industry. Textile producers were concerned that the Canadian government was considering a tariff-rebate scheme for their clothing industry. Some automakers believed that the agreement was too slow in phasing out Canadian duty remissions intended to encourage the use of Canadian auto parts by foreign-owned manufacturers in Canada. At the time the trade pact was being considered in Congress, an omnibus trade bill was in conference, thus slowing down the process.[53]

Despite the opposition, there were powerful sources of support as well. The National Association of Manufacturers and the American Business Conference spoke in behalf of the measure in testimony before the House Ways and Means Committee. Top congressional leaders agreed with administration officials that legislation would not be formally introduced before June 1 and would not include substantive changes in the pact.[54]

By the middle of May, the House Ways and Means Committee and the Senate Finance Committee had informally worked out versions of the trade bills after consulting with officials of the office of U.S. trade representative. The Senate Finance Committee wanted to add provisions designed to placate suspicious senators, such as John Danforth (Republican, Missouri) and John Heinz (Republican, Pennsylvania). It stipulated that the agreement couldn't formally go into effect until the president determines that Canada had taken steps to ensure compliance by provincial and local governments. The Finance Committee also added a requirement that American members of the binational panel that would be established to settle disputes would have to be confirmed by the U.S. Senate.[55]

On May 26, differences between the House and Senate versions of legislation were largely resolved through an informal conference. Through the unusual process of informal negotiations, the Reagan administration sought to overcome obstacles even before the bill was formally introduced.[56]

The conference negotiators decided to compromise on the question of confirmation of members of panels concerned with settling disputes on subsidies and dumping (selling products below cost). In order to prevent delays in starting the panels, it was agreed that the roster of citizens from which American members would be drawn would be subject to review by the Finance and Ways and Means Committees. They also agreed that binational panel decisions should be binding on U.S. government agencies. They could not agree on a Finance Committee recommendation that the president must determine that the Canadian government has taken steps to ensure provincial compliance before the pact would go into effect;

disagreement also persisted on a provision proposed by Senator George J. Mitchell (Democrat, Maine) that imported lobsters must meet U.S. rules barring the taking of undersized crustaceans. These matters had to be left to the administration to decide separately.[57]

Concern with imported uranium persisted among some western senators. However, a ruling by the U.S. Supreme Court on June 15, 1988, stated that the Atomic Energy Act did not require the Department of Energy to impose limits on imports of uranium ore, unless such restrictions would revive the American industry. Domestic producers had insisted that the law mandated import restrictions.[58]

On July 25, the president formally submitted legislation to carry out the trade pact. By August 9, the House had overwhelmingly passed the bill by a vote of 366 to 40. On September 19, the Senate voted 83 to 9 in favor of the measure.[59]

The key provisions of the trade agreement approved by Congress would phase out all tariffs between the two countries over the next 10 years; ensure that American and Canadian businesses would be free of discriminatory provincial and state laws; loosen Canadian restrictions on American investment; ensure free trade in financial services, such as banking; guarantee equal United States access to Canadian energy sources; tighten "rules of origin" for determining whether enough of a product is made in the United States or Canada to qualify for duty-free treatment under government procurement rules; create new binational panels to decide appeals in disputed cases of dumping and determine countervailing duties that are used against dumping; and establish a United States–Canada Trade Commission to oversee implementation of the agreement and deal with other disputes.[60]

The consideration of the measure in Canada indicates the importance of the federal and parliamentary institutions of that country. The Canadian provinces, roughly comparable to American states, are important political and legal entities. The governments of the provinces could generate support for, or opposition to, the pact. The Liberal premier of Ontario, the largest province and the center of much of the manufacturing and financial interests of the nation, spoke out against it, suggesting that it threatened domestic jobs and businesses.[61] The government of Quebec, the second most populous province, was much more favorably inclined to the agreement because it was seen as promoting trade and economic development.[62]

The Conservatives had a substantial majority in the popularly elected house of Parliament, and the Canadian House of Commons approved the pact on August 31 by a vote of 177 to 64. Nevertheless, opposition parties insisted that the government call national elections to decide the question of free trade. The Senate, which was under Liberal control, had made clear late in July that it would not consider the government legislation until Prime Minister Mulroney called new elections.[63]

After elections were scheduled for November, the agreement became the centerpiece of the struggle between Mulroney, Liberal leader John Turner, and New Democratic party leader Edward Broadbent. Many of the objections that had already been voiced by critics of the free-trade agreement resurfaced. Arguments that water and energy sources would be diverted to the United States, that Canadian labor and business would suffer, and that Canada's independence and national identity would be undermined were raised by opposition politicians.[64]

The Conservatives countered that the agreement adequately protected Canadian interests. They argued that thousands of new jobs would be created as a result of free trade and that Canada would prosper in the years ahead.[65]

The November elections led to a solid Conservative victory, albeit with a slightly reduced majority in the House of Commons. By December 1988, both houses of Parliament had approved the free-trade agreement.[66]

The free-trade pact shows how the reduction or elimination of subsidies can be used as a means of aiding business. Inherent in this process was not only a consideration of broad issues—the desirability of enlarged markets, the protection of Canadian sovereignty—but also the resolution of a number of specific issues, such as the continuation or elimination of public subsidies, the importation of energy sources, and the mechanism for resolving conflicts.

This agreement illustrates the possibility of cooperation between the executive and legislative branches even before the formal process of legislative consideration has begun. Although law-making could have become a contest of wills between the two houses of Congress and the agreement might have fallen prey to the suspicions or hostility of the many interests fearful of the lowering of trade barriers, there was adequate bipartisan support to prevent this from happening.

Of course, reducing obstacles to free trade also requires a willingness to take into account foreign concerns. Unless the environment is conducive and leadership is present in other countries, this option will not be available to American policy-makers.

SUMMARY

Subsidies take many forms, and they can be either direct or indirect in nature. Direct subsidies are payments and material benefits granted for the purpose of promoting or assisting certain activities. Indirect subsidies include taxes or regulations designed to aid certain actors by reducing competition or giving them an advantage over others.

Advocates of subsidies insist that they are necessary in order to prevent market failure; maintain national security; assist new industries; develop human capital; and prevent adverse effects on producers, workers, or consumers. Opponents of subsidies argue that they interfere with the efficient operations of the market, and they question the equity of aiding some actors rather than others.

We considered two different approaches to helping business that were tried by the federal government in recent years. The first, the loan guarantee to Chrysler, coupled with tax relief and limits on Japanese automobile imports, helped to save a large American corporation from financial collapse. The free-trade agreement between the United States and Canada attempts to assist producers and investors by reducing or eliminating subsidies, tariffs, and other obstacles to trade. It is probably not coincidental that the trade pact was actively pursued by an administration that also favored deregulation in many areas of the economy.

The Chrysler bailout and the free-trade agreement are metaphors respectively for state intervention and free-market economics. In the final chapter we will consider these conflicting views of the role of government in the economy as we examine some of the problems facing our country in the years ahead.

NOTES

[1]Cited in Charles Woolsey Cole, *Colbert and a Century of French Mercantilism*, vol. 1 (Hamden, CT: Archon Books, 1964), p. 343.

[2]For a discussion of subsidies, see John H. Mutti, *Taxes, Subsidies and Competitiveness Internationally* (Washington, DC: NPA, 1982)

[3]James D. Forman, *Capitalism: Economic Individualism to Today's Welfare State* (New York: New Viewpoints, 1973), pp. 12–15; and Fernand Braudel, *The Wheels of Commerce: Civilization and Capitalism, 15th-18th Century*, vol. 2 (New York: Harper & Row, Pub. 1979), pp. 542–549, 554.

[4]See, for example, *Farm Policy: The Politics of Soil, Surpluses, and Subsidies* (Washington, DC: Congressional Quarterly, 1984), pp. 105–107, 110.

[5]National security considerations have also played a part in subsidies to the maritime industry. See Gerald R. Jantscher, *Bread upon the Waters: Federal Aids to the Maritime Industries* (Washington, DC: Brookings Institution, 1975).

[6] "Alexander Hamilton's Final Version of The Report on the Subject of Manufactures," *The Papers of Alexander Hamilton*, vol 10, ed. Harold C. Syrett (New York: Columbia University Press, 1966), p. 268.

[7]See Theodore W. Schultz, "Investment in Human Capital," *American Economic Review*, 51 (March 1961), 1–17; and Jacob Mincer, *Schooling, Experience and Earnings* (New York: Columbia University Press, 1974).

[8]See the remarks of Paul E. Peterson, "Federalism and the Great Society: Political Perspectives on Poverty Research," in *Poverty and Public Policy: An Evaluation of Social Science Research*, ed. Vincent T. Covello (Boston: G. K. Hall, 1980), pp. 273–275.

[9]Milton Friedman and Rose Friedman, *Free to Choose: A Personal Statement* (New York: Harcourt Brace Jovanovich, 1980), pp. 45–46, 51–52.

[10]On the power of private interests, see Grants McConnell, *Private Power and American Democracy* (New York: Knopf, 1966), particularly Chapter 10; and Duane Lockard, *The Perverted Priorities of American Politics* (New York: Macmillan, 1971), pp. 77–79, 149–155.

[11]Michael Moritz and Barrett Seaman, *Going for Broke: The Chrysler Story* (Garden City, NY: Doubleday, 1981), pp. 178–179, 186–189, and 222–245.

[12]*Ibid.*, pp. 248–251.

[13]*Congress and the Nation: 1977–1980* (Washington, DC: Congressional Quarterly, 1981), p. 283; and Robert B. Reich and John D. Donahue, *New Deals: The Chrysler Revival and the American System* (New York: Times Books, 1985), p. 88.

[14]*Congress and the Nation: 1977–1980*, p. 281.

[15]*Ibid.*

[16]*Ibid.*

[17]*Ibid.*

[18]*Ibid.*

[19]*Ibid.*, p. 282.

[20]*Ibid.*; and Moritz and Seaman, p. 282.

[21]*Congress and the Nation: 1977–1980*, p. 282.

[22]*Ibid.*

[23]*Ibid.*

[24]*Ibid.*

[25]*Ibid.*

[26]*Ibid.*

[27]*Ibid.*, pp. 282, 284.

[28]Reich and Donahue, pp. 222–237.

[29]*Ibid.*, pp. 238, 242.

[30]*Ibid.*, p. 238.

[31]*Ibid.*, pp. 242–244.

[32]*Ibid.*, pp. 244–245.

[33]*Ibid.*, p. 245.

[34]*Ibid.*, p. 246.

[35]*Ibid.*, pp. 254, 256.

[36]*Ibid.*, pp. 254–256.

[37]*Ibid.*, p. 283.

[38]Jeffrey J. Schott, "The Free Trade Agreement: A U.S. Assessment" in *The Canada–United States Free Trade Agreement: The Global Impact*, eds. Jeffrey J. Schott and Murray G. Smith (Washington, DC: Institute for International Economics, 1988), p. 9.

[39]Alan M. Rugman, "Multinationals and the Free Trade Agreement," in *Trade-Offs on Free Trade: The Canada–U.S. Free Trade Agreement*, eds. Marc Gold and David Leyton-Brown (Toronto: Carswell, 1988), pp. 7–8.

[40]For a good overview of economic relations between Canada and the United States, see Richard G. Lipsey, "Canada and the United States: The Economic Dimension," in *Canada and the United States: Enduring Friendship, Persistent*

Stress, eds. Charles F. Doran and John H. Sigler (Englewood Cliffs, NJ: Prentice Hall, 1985), pp. 69–108.

[41]*Congressional Quarterly Almanac, 1980* (Washington, DC: Congressional Quarterly, 1981), p. 82-B.

[42]Stephen Clarkson, *Canada and the Reagan Challenge: Crisis and Adjustment, 1981–85* (Toronto: James Lorimar, 1985), pp. 359–361.

[43] "Walkout from the Talks," *Maclean's* (October 5, 1987), 17; and Steven Pressman, "Larger Issues Almost Derail Canada Trade Talks," *Congressional Quarterly Weekly Report* (April 26, 1986), 905–906.

[44] "Walkout from the Talks," p. 17.

[45]*Ibid.*, pp. 14–17.

[46]A. W. Johnson, "Free Trade and Cultural Industries"; Malcolm Lester, "Free Trade and Canadian Book Publishing"; and Rick Salutin, "Culture and the Deal: Another Broken Promise," in *Trade-Offs on Free Trade*, pp. 350–369. See also "Skepticism in the Arts," *Maclean's* (October 19, 1987), 21.

[47]Philip K. Verlenger, Jr., "Implications of the Energy Provisions," in *The Canada–United States Free Trade Agreement*, pp. 117–127.

[48]Paul Wonnacott, "The Auto Sector," in *The Canada–United States Free Trade Agreement*, pp. 101–109.

[49]Murray G. Smith, "Services in the Canada–U.S. Free Trade Agreement"; and Andre Saumier, "The Canada–U.S. Free Trade Agreement and the Services Sector," in *Trade-Offs on Free Trade*, pp. 295–303 and 323–331.

[50] "Free Trade and Cultural Industries," in *Trade-Offs on Free Trade*, pp. 350–360; Jeffrey J. Schott and Murray G. Smith, "Services and Investment," and J. H. Warren, "Comments," in *The Canada–United States Free Trade Agreement*, pp. 137–150, 153–158.

[51] "Redrawing the Nation," *Maclean's* (October 19, 1987), 14–17.

[52]"U.S.–Canada Free-Trade Agreement Signed," *Congressional Quarterly Weekly Report* (January 9, 1988), 87.

[53]Bruce Stokes, "Big Sky Country's Doubts About Ottawa," *National Journal* (February 27, 1988), 546–547; Elizabeth Wehr, "U.S.–Canada Pact Draws Fire on Hill," *Congressional Quarterly Weekly Report* (February 13, 1988), 305; and "U.S.–Canada Free-Trade Pact Seen Likely to Win Approval," *Congressional Quarterly Weekly Report* (March 5, 1988), 581–582.

[54] "U.S.–Canada Free-Trade Pact Seen Likely to Win Approval," p. 582.

[55] "House Panel Starts Work on U.S.–Canada Pact," *Congressional Quarterly Weekly Report* (May 7, 1988), 1261; Elizabeth Wehr, "Smooth Start in Both Chambers for U.S.–Canada Trade Accord," *Congressional Quarterly Weekly Report* (May 14, 1988), 1276; and Elizabeth Wehr, "Senate, House Panels Draft Canada Trade Bill," *Congressional Quarterly Weekly Report* (May 21, 1988), 1363–1364.

[56]Elizabeth Wehr, "Conferees OK U.S.–Canada Trade Proposals," *Congressional Quarterly Weekly Report* (May 28, 1988), 1446.

[57]*Ibid.*

[58] "Ruling Erases One Problem of U.S.–Canada Pact," *Congressional Quarterly Weekly Report* (June 18, 1988), 1705.

[59]Elizabeth Wehr, "Canada Trade Pact Gets Strong Support in House," *Congressional Quarterly Weekly Report* (August 13, 1988), 2278; and Elizabeth Wehr, "Senate Clears Bill on Canada–Free Trade Pact," *Congressional Quarterly Weekly Report* (September 24, 1988), 2665.

[60]*Ibid.*

[61] "The Battle for Ontario," *Maclean's* (October 3, 1988), 13–14; and "Interview with Ontario Premier David R. Peterson," *New York Times* (June 27, 1988), section 4, p. 10.

[62] "Notes Pour Une Allocution de M. Jean-Claude Villiard, Sous-Ministre des Affaires Internationales Devant The Committee on Canada–United States Relations," Quebec City, Quebec, October 3, 1988; and Barbara McDougall, "Political Perspectives," in *The Canada–United States Free Trade Agreement*, p. 181.

[63] "Canada Trade Bill Signed," *Congressional Quarterly Weekly Report* (October 1, 1988), 2718.

[64]*Congressional Quarterly Almanac 1988* (Washington, DC: Congressional Quarterly, 1989), p. 228; and "Anatomy of an Election," *Maclean's* (December 5, 1988), 21–23. Although the New Democratic party continued to oppose the free-trade agreement, most of the vocal arguments against it during the campaign were raised by the Liberals.

[65] "A Critical Debate," *Maclean's* (October 24, 1988), 13; and "Straight to the Heart," *Maclean's* (November 14, 1988), 12–15.

[66] "Free-Trade Accord Clears Its Final Hurdle in Canada," *New York Times* (December 31, 1988) 17.

CHAPTER EIGHT

Conclusions

> The Congress shall have power to lay and collect taxes, duties, imports and excises, to pay the debts and provide for the common defense and general welfare of the United States ... to borrow money on the credit of the United States; to regulate commerce with foreign nations and among the several states, and with the Indian tribes; to establish ... uniform laws on the subject of bankruptcies, ... to coin money, regulate the value thereof, and of foreign coin, and fix the standards of weights and measures ....
>
> *U.S. Constitution, Article I, Section 8*

THE ECONOMIC TOOLS OF GOVERNMENT

We have examined five major tools used by the national government in making economic policy: spending, taxing, monetary expansion and contraction, regulation, and subsidies. Each of these means of managing the economy has certain strengths and weaknesses.

Government expenditures can serve as a stimulus to the economy, and a reduction in spending can be used to curb inflation. However, it is often difficult to fine-tune the level of government outlays. For example, if an attempt is made to reduce inflation by cutting federal spending, it is possible that recessionary pressures will be accelerated and unemployment will grow. A growth in unemployment will lead to increased levels of social welfare spending, partially negating the lower levels of federal expenditures. Much of the cost of increased welfare outlays will have to be borne by state and local governments.

Both the level of spending and the effects of specific kinds of expenditures are difficult to adjust. Dollars spent for weapons development and procurement are likely to be of the most immediate benefit to defense contractors in selected communities. Not only will those companies and the communities in which they are located be harmed if expenditures are severely reduced for this purpose, but so also will the engineers, scientists, and skilled workers who are employed by the firms in question. Of course, most social welfare programs have different beneficiaries and target populations who will be affected by increases or declines in public spending.

Taxation involves more than raising money to meet public needs. It can be used to stimulate investment, reduce private spending, and generally reward or penalize certain behaviors. There is, however, no agreement as to the appropriate rate of taxation, the mix of taxes, or even whether the tax system is a suitable mechanism for altering private economic choices.

The Federal Reserve System plays a crucial role in the nation's economy. The expansion and contraction of the money supply can either stimulate purchases and investments or reduce inflation by curbing economic growth. Unfortunately, sharp increases in the amount of money are likely to cause prices to mount, while significant cuts in available credit will have an adverse effect on farmers, businessowners, and workers.

Regulation serves to protect people from the inadequacies of the marketplace, but it also adds to the cost of doing business and even reduces competition. Similarly, subsidies, whether direct or indirect, help to protect producers and their employees from adverse economic forces, but they do so by favoring certain actors and increasing the cost of the goods produced. Clearly, actions that increase prices or reduce competition have some negative effects on consumers.

MEETING FUTURE CHALLENGES: ECONOMIC COMPETITION

Although we can agree that the economic tools at the disposal of the federal government are imperfect, we must ask whether they can be used to meet the challenges facing the United States in the years ahead. Two of the most serious economic problems confronting the nation today are maintaining its economic competitiveness and permitting all members of the work force to share in its growing wealth.

Immediately after the Second World War, the United States was by far the wealthiest and most productive actor in the international marketplace. Over half of the value of all goods and services produced throughout the world originated in this country. By the 1980s, the American economy was generating approximately one-fourth of the wealth created by all members of the world community.[1]

The decline in America's preeminent position was hardly surprising. We had survived the war without the destruction encountered by the European powers and Japan. In the four decades following the war these countries had rebuilt their economies and become our great competitors. Moreover, new industrial forces in the Third World were growing in strength; South Korea and Taiwan had become nations to be reckoned with.

Nevertheless, the new role of the United States was precarious and in some ways embarrassing. Year after year we ran huge trade deficits. America became the largest debtor in the world, kept afloat by the influx of foreign loans to our public and private sectors. Although we created more new jobs than the members of the Common Market during the 1980s and experienced an unusually long period of economic growth after the recession of 1981 and 1982, the growth in productivity was far less impressive.[2] It was unclear whether the United States could successfully respond to the new strength of Western Europe as it became more economically unified in 1992.

Can the federal government use public policy initiatives to help make the United States more economically competitive? Much depends on how we analyze the causes of the current dilemma.

There are at least three major elements of our reduced capacity to compete economically. The public policy component includes those actions that government takes, or fails to take, that affect productivity. For example, persistently high deficit spending and tax policies that discourage savings adversely influence investments needed for modernization of plants and equipment. The management component deals with the practices of private-sector owners and managers that affect the quantity or quality of production. Thus, poor labor–management relations and a failure to institute careful quality-control procedures may lead to lax standards of workmanship. The cultural aspect concerns those skills and values that have an impact on the quality and quantity of work. The level of education and acquired skills, standards of honesty, and adherence to the work ethic all help to determine the ability of employees to do their job and the quality of their performance.[3]

In order to see how government policy might affect economic competition, we should examine three specific reasons that have been suggested for a decline of American economic dominance. These three factors—insufficient personal savings, a mediocre educational system, and a reduced emphasis on the quality of the goods we produce and the services we deliver—illustrate the elements that we have identified.

Increasing Personal Savings

The rate of personal savings during the 1980s has generally varied from 3 percent to no more than 6 percent. By way of comparison, in Western Europe and Japan, citizens generally save approximately 10 to 20 percent of their personal income. The low rate of savings has limited the amount of funds available for investment in American business.[4] The continuing high level of federal deficits has exacerbated this tendency because a growing share of the limited funds set aside for savings is used to pay for U.S. government securities. The burgeoning public debt has also meant that more of our resources have had to go to interest payments, rather than to more productive investments in education or in meeting the needs of our people for better transportation and an adequate supply of safe water.[5] Clearly, more of the federal budget and a higher proportion of the gross national product (GNP)—the value of goods and services we produce—has been allocated to servicing the national debt (See Table 8–1).

TABLE 8–1 Interest Payments on the Federal Debt, Fiscal Years 1980–1989

Year	Interest Payments (in billions of dollars)	Percentage of Federal Outlays	Percentage of GNP
1980	52.5	8.9	2.0
1981	68.7	10.1	2.3
1982	85.0	11.4	2.7
1983	89.8	11.1	2.7
1984	111.1	13.0	3.0
1985	129.4	13.7	3.3
1986	136.0	13.7	3.2
1987	138.6	13.8	3.1
1988	151.7	14.3	3.2
1989	169.1	14.8	3.3

Source: Executive Office of the President, Office of Management and Budget, *Historical Tables: Budget of the United States Government, Fiscal Year 1990* (Washington, DC: U.S. Government Printing office, 1989), pp. 43, 44, 50, 51; and *Budget, Fiscal Year 1991* (Washington, DC: U.S. Government Printing Office, 1990), p. A-294.

Defenders of the status quo point to the fact that deficits have declined since the passage of the Gramm-Rudman-Hollings law, which we discussed in Chapter Three. Moreover, the growth of employment suggests a vigorous economy, one not hindered by the need to borrow money for the operations of the federal government. The influx of money from foreign countries is an indicator of confidence in our economy, not a warning sign that we are on the skids.[6]

Unfortunately, this optimistic vision of the current situation overlooks some unpleasant facts. First, the official budgetary deficits do not count large off-budget obligations of the U.S. government, such as the huge payments to the savings and loan industry, which may cost taxpayers $200 billion to $500 billion in the next 30 years (estimates vary widely).[7]

Second, although there has been significant growth in employment, most of that growth has occurred in part-time or low-wage service jobs.[8] Perhaps if more money were available for capital investment, we would have created better-paying full-time positions in the industrial sector, thus helping to maintain our competitive position in manufacturing.

Third, foreign investments in the United States have a capacity both to help and to injure the nation's economy. Few would deny that it is better for a foreign-owned company to build a plant in our country or to put more capital in a weak American firm than to see our businesses fail or to have jobs exported elsewhere. On the other hand, much money from overseas has been invested in real estate or to buy well-established corporations. Will such changes increase the productivity of our workers or assist in the growth of employment and income? While it is true that we can neither exclude the movement of foreign capital to our shores nor seek self-sufficiency in an international economy increasingly dominated by multinational corporations, we must recognize that growing dependency on foreign investment makes us vulnerable to the export of profits, the decisions of other governments, which control companies headquartered in their territories, and the loss of capital whenever changes in the value of the dollar make it less profitable to invest here rather than in other rapidly growing nations.[9]

We could improve the level of American savings through various changes in public policy. Three of the most common proposals center around alterations in federal tax law. A reduction in the rates of the capital gains tax, some have argued, will encourage more people to invest in our businesses, since the profits from the sale of stocks or bonds will be treated more favorably than ordinary income.[10] A second option is to treat savings differently from earned income. Thus, Individual Retirement Accounts (IRAs) or even funds deposited in banks and other thrift institutions could provide savers with tax credits (offsets against the money owed to the Internal Revenue Service) or with deductions for the interest earned.[11] The most far-reaching suggestion is for the imposition of a consumption tax with broad coverage. Whether a value-added tax (VAT) similar to that found in most advanced Western countries—one imposed on the incremental value of goods and services at each level of production and exchange—or a national sales tax like the levies collected in almost all of our states, a consumption tax would provide a disincentive for people to spend money rather than save it.[12]

Each of these options has benefits as well as adverse effects. Most people would agree that encouraging savings and investment are desirable goals and might be assisted by modifications of existing tax laws. However, the first two changes would partially undo the effects of the 1986 Tax Reform Act by reintroducing additional tax shelters and unequal rates of income taxation. More favorable treatment of capital gains would not necessarily provide additional investment for new companies or for the purchase of new plant and equipment by existing firms. Capital gains income is most often derived from the sale of securities issued years ago by companies long established or from real estate and other forms of property not directly involved in improving productivity. IRAs may encourage long-term savings, but the extent of the additional funds generated by IRAs is difficult to estimate. Undoubtedly, much of the money for these accounts is merely transferred from savings deposits or short-term instruments.[13] Sales taxes and VATs are regressive, imposing higher burdens on those with low income. They also add to the cost of living by imposing higher prices on the goods and services that we purchase.[14]

Improving Educational Performance

In a report entitled *A Nation at Risk*, a presidential commission appointed by Ronald Reagan spoke of the "rising tide of mediocrity" that was engulfing American education.[15] Politicians and business leaders have voiced concern about the harm done to the nation's economy by inadequately educated employees entering the work-place.[16]

Evidence of the relatively low level of educational achievement in this country is all too apparent. International assessments of knowledge of math and science show American students lagging well behind their counterparts in Europe, Japan, and other industrialized countries.[17] Despite our boasts about the egalitarian aspects of American public education, Japan now graduates a higher proportion of its students from high school than we do. It also trains more engineers.[18]

It would be simplistic to say that there is a perfect correlation between a country's educational standards and its economic productivity. However, a technically oriented society requires that many workers have a high level of mathematical and scientific knowledge. As service and professional jobs become more sophisticated, it will probably also be necessary for people to be able to read and understand increasingly complex written materials. To the extent that students in other nations have more knowledge and skill in these vital areas, they are likely to be better able to operate more effectively in highly competitive international markets.

If education is of importance to the future prosperity of the United States, what can the federal government do to improve the quality of schooling? Additional funds could be provided for education at all levels, and attempts might be made to establish national performance standards for students and teachers. Monies could be targeted at areas of special need, including preschool education, mathematical and scientific instruction, and the training of engineers and technicians.[19]

There are undoubtedly formidable obstacles to the improvement of education through the means that have been suggested. For the most part, educational decisions are made by state and local governments. Even the educational conference called by President Bush in 1989 failed to recommend the imposition of national standards, though it accepted the concept of goals or objectives that the states should try to meet.[20]

Not all critics of American education believe that lack of money is the primary problem facing our schools. Rather, they argue that cultural factors have led to relatively low levels of educational achievement. Broken families and widespread undervaluing of learning and intellectual accomplishment, it is suggested, have played a critical role in reducing the success of our students.[21]

Clearly, the evidence is mixed. High-achieving students can, and do, graduate from financially weak schools. On the other hand, school districts that have more money to spend on their students often have lower dropout rates and a higher proportion of their graduates attending college.[22] Given the continued high level of deficit spending, any additional federal funds will probably have to be allocated to areas of critical need or tied to improved performance by students and teachers.

Improving the Quality of Goods and Services

A common complaint concerning our economic output is that we often produce goods and services of inferior quality. An emphasis on securing quick profits sometimes leads to laxity in the standards of production. Thus, whether management or labor is mainly responsible, potential customers in the United States and elsewhere will increasingly turn to others for the items and technical services they wish to purchase.[23]

The validity of the complaint regarding the quality of American products and services is challenged by some observers. It is difficult to secure empirical evidence about the qualitative failures of the wide array of goods and services we produce. Moreover, it is not clear whether quality or price is the primary reason that customers shun American-made products. It should be noted that our balance of trade has improved since the value of the dollar declined from its high levels of the mid-1980s. Even if low quality is an important reason for the relative lack of success in selling our goods to potential customers, efforts are already being made to improve our standards in the workplace. For example, some companies have developed quality circles among their employees, and they actively solicit suggestions to reduce mistakes in production.[24]

It is clear that the role of the federal government in improving quality will be marginal unless we are willing to accept much more widespread supervision and regulation of private firms. A more likely alternative is for the national authorities to encourage higher standards of excellence by disseminating information on what companies are doing to improve quality or for federal agencies to distribute awards to businesses that have made major improvements in quality control.

SHARING THE NATION'S WEALTH

At a time of rapid economic expansion, the issue of whether there has been a slight shift in the distribution of wealth may seem to be of little concern. Most groups within the population are likely to share in the nation's growing prosperity. However, the economic growth we have experienced since the end of the recession of 1982 has not been so dramatic. Average annual growth in GNP has been less than 3 percent in real dollar terms (i.e., dollars adjusted for inflation). Much of the growth in employment has been in part-time jobs, and there are fewer people working in the manufacturing sector now than there were in the late 1970s.[25]

The number of people living below the poverty line has declined only slightly since the recession, and there are proportionately more people in low-income groups today than at any time since the late 1940s.[26] Economic conditions vary widely throughout the country, and many states that now have a smaller share of output originating in manufacturing have shown a relative reduction in per capita income (Table 8–2).

TABLE 8–2 States with a Lower Share of Output Originating in Manufacturing*, Comparing per Capita Personal Income in 1967 and 1986

States	Per Capita Income as a Percentage of the National per Capita Personal Income, 1967	Per Capita Income as a percentage of the National per Capita Personal Income, 1986
West Virginia	73.5	72.5
Connecticut	125.9	133.8
New Jersey	116.5	128.7
Pennsylvania	100.5	97.8
Maryland	108.4	115.9
Montana	87.8	80.3
Illinois	118.8	106.1
New York	121.1	115.2
Delaware	115.1	106.1
Indiana	100.9	89.9
Michigan	107.2	101.4
Washington	107.3	101.8
Wyoming	93.8	87.1
Ohio	101.4	94.9
Kentucky	76.5	77.1

*States with a lower share of output originating in manufacturing in 1986 than in 1967.

Sources:Gerald A. Carlino, "What Can Output Measures Tell Us about Deindustrialization in the Nation and Its Regions?" *Business Review—Federal Reserve Bank of Philadelphia* (January/February 1989), 21; and U.S. Bureau of the Census, *Statistical Abstract of the United States: 1969*, p. 320, and *Statistical Abstract of the United States: 1989*, p. 433.

The federal government could take action to reduce inequalities among the states and among the various income groups in the nation. It could increase expenditures for the training of less skilled and more frequently unemployed workers. Funding for the training of workers has significantly declined during the 1980s.[27] States or metropolitan areas that have persistently high levels of unemployment could be given assistance to provide public-service jobs for the more vulnerable members of the workforce.

Critics of these proposals question whether they are necessary. They point to the creation of millions of new jobs during the 1980s and suggest that we will probably have a labor shortage in the near future as a result of low birth rates and an aging population.

The fact remains that there are many new entrants into the workforce who possess very limited skills. They will have difficulty finding good jobs as the economy becomes more complex. Moreover, high levels of poverty, particularly in the central cities of many metropolitan areas, indicate that growing productivity has not led to a more widespread sharing of the nation's wealth.

TWO APPROACHES FOR THE PUBLIC SECTOR

As we examine the economic problems confronting the United States, we must also consider two opposing approaches that have been proposed for dealing with them. One emphasizes the importance of the marketplace in making decisions, while the other focuses on the role of government.

The Reagan administration's emphasis on deregulation, tax relief for individuals (particularly those in the upper income brackets), and a reduction in subsidies and trade barriers exemplifies the free-market approach. This approach has been broadly supported by such economists as Milton Friedman and Arthur Laffer. Although their premises are not always alike, free-market advocates tend to see government as more of a hindrance than a help to increased economic productivity. They view most efforts to redistribute wealth through means other than individual initiative or private charity as harmful and self-defeating.[28]

The creation of an industrial policy is an approach advocated by Robert Reich and Lester Thurow, among others. They believe that in a highly competitive international economy it is essential that our country have a carefully crafted strategy for advancing our collective economic interests. Industrial policies try to promote industrial growth and efficiency. Supporters of this approach argue that Japan and the more prosperous countries of Western Europe have devised such strategies, and that all countries in fact have policies to help their chief industries, whether or not they are clearly formulated and explicitly stated.

Specifically, advocates of an industrial policy wish to use taxes, regulations, and subsidies to assist in the modernization of American industry, the training of workers, and the generation of capital needed for economic development, particularly in areas in which the economy has foundered. Some supporters argue that the federal government should also choose a few industries that are vital to our economic well-being and that show potential for growth and give them special aid.[29]

There are criticisms voiced of both the free-market approach and industrial policy. The collapse of many savings and loan institutions even as deregulation was in vogue suggests that loosening government restrictions is not always the answer to promoting greater prosperity. The continuation of high levels of poverty and growing evidence of homelessness and hunger indicate that free-market economics does not prevent significant human suffering.[30]

Opponents of industrial policy argue that it is unnecessary and potentially harmful. Given the fairly steady economic growth since the end of the recession in the early 1980s, it is unnecessary for the national government to intervene actively in the making of major economic decisions. The marketplace, they assert, has proven to be an adequate mechanism for creating millions of new jobs, improving productivity, and curbing the high inflation rates that had previously prevailed. If federal authorities tried to influence where monies should be invested or what industries should be subsidized or aided through the tax system, decisions would probably be less rational than those made by self-interested investors and entrepreneurs. Indeed, decisions might well be determined by interest-group pressures, constituency considerations, or campaign contributions. Government, it is said, is not capable of picking "winners" and "losers."[31]

In all probability, policies to improve our competitive position in the world or to reduce economic inequalities will require piecemeal changes. Coalitions must be formed to bring together opposing interest groups and government officials of different parties and ideologies. Even with strong presidential leadership, basic economic change will be difficult to achieve. Without such leadership, the likelihood of molding coalitions for meaningful change is negligible.

NOTES

[1]Norman R. Augustine, "U.S. Credibility and Viability in Worldwide Competition." Address delivered to the Conference Board Public Affairs Conference, New York, May 25, 1989. Published in *Vital Speeches of the Day*, 55 (September 1, 1989), 694.

[2]Robert B. Reich, "The Economics of Illusion and the Illusion of Economics," *Foreign Affairs*, 66 (1988), 516–528; and Benjamin M. Friedman, *Day of Reckoning: The Consequences of American Economic Policy Under Reagan and After* (New York: Random House, 1988).

[3] "Final Report of the Seventy-fourth American Assembly," in Martin K. Starr, ed., *Global Competitiveness: Getting the U.S. Back on Track* (New York: W. W. Norton & Co., 1988), pp. 299–310.

[4]For information on earlier patterns of savings, see Thomas K. McCraw, "From Partners to Competitors: An Overview of the Period Since World War II," and Michael G. Rukstad, "Fiscal Policy and Business–Government Relation," in *America Versus Japan*, ed. Thomas K. McCraw (Boston: Harvard Business School Press, 1986), pp. 14, 324. Also, see William D. Nordhaus, "What's Wrong with a Declining National Saving Rate?" *Challenge* (July/August 1989), 22–26.

[5]For information on the need for infrastructure improvement, see Friedman, pp. 7, 204–205.

[6]"As the Reagan Era Ends: An Appraisal and an Appreciation," *Nation's Business* (December 1988), 67; and Rich Thomas, "The Magic of Reaganomics," *Newsweek* (December 26, 1988), 40–1ff.

[7]James R. Barth and Michael G. Bradley, "The Ailing S & Ls: Causes and Cures," *Challenge* (March/April 1989), 30–38; John R. Cranford, "How Much Will a Bailout Cost? It Depends on Whom You Ask," *Congressional Quarterly Weekly* (May 27, 1989), 1245–1246; and Paul Starobin, "Thanks A Lot, Joe!" *National Journal* (June 23, 1990), 1568.

[8]Susan E. Shank and Steven E. Haugen, "The Employment Situation During 1986: Job Gains Continue, Unemployment Dips," *Monthly Labor Review*, 110 (February 1987), 3–10; and Wayne J. Howe and William Parks II, "Labor

Market Completes Sixth Year of Expansion in 1988," *Monthly Labor Review*, 112 (February 1989), 3–14.

[9]For different views of the value of foreign investment in the United States, see Jeffrey M. Schaefer and David G. Strongin, "Why All the Fuss About Foreign Investment," *Challenge* (May/June 1989), 31–35; and Martin Tolchin and Susan Tolchin, *Buying into America: How Foreign Money is Changing the Face of Our Nation* (New York: New York Times Books, 1988). Also see Keniche Ohmae, "Beyond Friction to Fact: The Borderless Economy," *New Perspectives Quarterly*, 7 (Spring 1990), 20–21.

[10]Elizabeth Wehr, "Bush's Capital Gains Plan Revives Old Debate," *Congressional Quarterly Weekly Report* (February 25, 1989), 369–372.

[11]Ronald D. Elving, "Bentsen's Counter: Restore IRAs," *Congressional Quarterly Weekly Report* (September 16, 1989), 2364.

[12]Elizabeth Wehr, "Country's Low Savings Rate Stirs Concern on Hill," *Congressional Quarterly Weekly Report* (April 22, 1989), 886.

[13]Ronald D. Elving, "Spotlight Turns to the Senate for Action on Capital Gains," *Congressional Quarterly Weekly Report* (September 30, 1989), 2533–2535.

[14]For two somewhat different views of the VAT, see Thomas J. Coyne, "Economic Impact of a State Value Added Tax," paper presented at the annual meeting of the Midwest Economic Association, Chicago, Illinois, April 22–24, 1971; and *The Value-Added Tax: Lessons from Europe*, ed. Henry J. Aaron (Washington, DC: Brookings Institution, 1981).

[15]National Commission on Excellence in Education, *A Nation At Risk: The Imperative for Educational Reform* (Washington, DC: U.S. Government Printing Office, 1982), p. 5.

[16]See, for example, David T. Kearns, "The United States Educational System: An Educational Recovery Plan," address delivered at the Economic Club of Detroit, Detroit, Michigan, October 26, 1987, published in *Vital Speeches of the Day*, 54 (December 15, 1987), 150–153; and Wallace T. Wilkinson, "Education Reform and Economic Competition," address delivered at St. Peter's College, Oxford, England, August 15, 1989, published in *Vital Speeches of the Day*, 56 (November 1, 1989), 40–43.

[17]R. A. Garden, "The Second IEA Mathematics Study," *Comparative Educational Review*, 31 (February 1987), 47–68; and Robert E. Yager and John E. Penick, "Resolving the Crisis in Science Education: Understanding Before Resolution," *Science Education*, 71 (January 1987), 49–55.

[18]U.S. Department of Education, *Japanese Education Today* (Washington, DC: U.S. Government Printing Office, 1987), pp. 7, 49–50.

[19] "Bush Education Proposal Draws Fire on Hill," *Congressional Quarterly Weekly Report* (April 8, 1989), 763; John Schacter and Phil Kuntz, "'Applied Technology' Programs Approved by House Panel," *Congressional Quarterly Weekly Report* (April 15, 1989), 825; and Phil Kuntz, "'Smart Start' for

Preschoolers Approved by Senate Labor," *Congressional Quarterly Weekly Report* (June 10, 1989), 1408.

[20] "A Summit for Schools," *Newsweek* (October 2, 1989), 56, 58; and "Bush, Governors Agree to Set School Goals," *Congressional Quarterly Weekly Report* (September 30, 1989), 2570.

[21]Amitai Etzioni, for example, argues that our educational resources are missallocated and that families often fail to develop traits and habits necessary for educational success. See his remarks in "School Reform: A Serious Challenge for Business," *Challenge* (May/June, 1989), 51–54. See also, *Japanese Education Today*, pp. 3–4, 69–70; and James S. Coleman, "'Social Capital' and Schools," *The Education Digest*, 53 (April 1988), 6–9.

[22]Russell S. Harrison, *Equality in Public School Finance* (Lexington, MA: Lexington Books, 1976), pp. 185–192; and Andrew Hahn, "Reaching Out to America's Dropouts: What to Do?" *Phi Delta Kappan*, 69 (December 1987), 256–263.

[23]George H. Conrades, "The Challenge of Global Competition," address delivered to the Akron Roundtable, Akron, Ohio, September 17, 1987, published in *Vital Speeches of the Day*, 54 (December 1, 1987), 125–128.

[24]Thomas J. Peters and Robert H. Waterman, Jr., *In Search of Excellence: Lessons from America's Best-Run Companies* (New York: Harper & Row, Pub., 1982).

[25]Shank and Haugen, "The Employment Situation During 1986"; Howe and Parks, "Labor Market Completes Sixth Year of Expansion in 1988." Also see Martin Neil Baily and Alok K. Chakrabarti, *Innovation and the Productivity Crisis* (Washington, DC: Brookings Institution, 1988) for possible explanations of low economic growth.

[26]Lester C. Thurow, " A Surge in Inequality," *Scientific American*, 256 (May 1987), 30–37.

[27]In 1980 the federal government spent approximately $10.3 billion on training and employment. That amount dropped to $5.2 billion in 1989. This reduction is particularly large when one takes into account increases in the cost of living and the provision of government services. Executive Office of the President, Office of Management and Budget, *Historical Tables: Budget of the United States Government, Fiscal Year 1989* (Washington, DC: U.S. Government Printing Office, 1988), pp. 65–67.

[28]Milton Friedman, *Capitalism and Freedom* (Chicago: University of Chicago Press, 1962:); *Foundations of Supply Side Economics: Theory and Evidence*, eds. Victor A. Canto, Douglas H. Joines, and Arthur B. Laffer (New York: Academic Press, 1982); and Jude Wanniski, *The Way the World Works: How Economies Fail and Succeed* (New York: Basic Books, 1978).

[29]*The Aims and Instruments of Industrial Policy: A Comparative Study* (Paris: Organisation for Economic Co-operation and Development, 1975); Ira C. Magaziner and Robert B. Reich, *Minding America's Business: The Decline*

and Rise of the American Economy (New York: Harcourt Brace Jovanovich, 1982); Robert Reich, "Industrial Policy," *New Republic* (March 21, 1982), 28–31; and Lester C. Thurow, *The Zero-Sum Solution* (New York: Simon & Schuster, 1985).

[30]Isabel V. Sawhill, "Reaganomics in Retrospect: Lessons for a New Administration," *Challenge* (May/June 1989), 57–59; and Robert Lekachman, *Visions and Nightmares: America After Reagan* (New York: Macmillan, 1987).

[31]Gerald A. Carlino, "What Can Output Measures Tell Us About Deindustrialization in the Nation and Its Regions?" *Business Review, Federal Reserve Bank of Philadelphia* (January/February 1989), 15–27; Paul Craig Roberts, "Supply-Side Economics and the Future," address delivered to the Conference on Reaganomics and Beyond, Institute for Economic Affairs, London, England, December 8, 1988, published in *Vital Speeches of the Day*, 55 (March 1, 1989), 307–309; William Darity, Jr., "The Managerial Class and Industrial Policy," *Industrial Relations*, 25 (Spring 1986), 212–227; and Russell L. Ackoff, Paul Broholm, and Roberta Snow, *Revitalizing Western Economies* (San Francisco: Jossey-Bass, 1984), pp. 47–54.

INDEX